YOU CAN
HEAR THEM KNOCKING

YOU CAN
HEAR THEM
KNOCKING

A STUDY IN
THE POLICING OF AMERICA

JOHN L. COOPER

Authors Choice Press

San Jose New York Lincoln Shanghai

You Can Hear Them Knocking
A Study in the Policing of America

Authors Choice Press
an imprint of iUniverse.com, Inc.

For information address:
iUniverse.com, Inc.
5220 S 16th, Ste. 200
Lincoln, NE 68512
www.iuniverse.com

Originally published by Kennikat Press

ISBN: 0-595-17034-X

Printed in the United States of America

CONTENTS

YOU CAN
HEAR THEM KNOCKING

ABOUT THE AUTHOR

John L. Cooper is Associate Professor of Sociology and Black Studies and Chairman of the Black Studies Department at John Jay College of Criminal Justice in New York City. A native of Philadelphia, he has long been interested in urban police problems. He is the author of *The Police and the Ghetto* (Kennikat Press, 1980).

1

MAINTAINING SOCIAL ORDER

In recent years, there have been many books written on the role of the police in American society. Yet it is safe to say that the true role of the police, and indeed the criminal justice system overall, is still largely misunderstood by the public and very likely by the people who make up its ranks. Perhaps this is due to the fact that we are all too willing to let the police, and the system, of which they are a part, define itself. It is self-evident that the law enforcement establishment would have the public believe that its primary function is that of crime fighting as a basic means of maintaining law and order. However, self-portraits can be misleading and self serving. For instance, while the public is persuaded to see the police as the managers of law and order, the police at the same time can promulgate the myth that they are but a ministerial force that works for full enforcement of all laws against all lawbreakers. In fact, the police exercise a great deal of discretion in their law enforcement procedures.

Moreover, the self-evaluations that are made by the law enforcement establishment tend to revolve around functional analyses, and these analyses tend to seek out causal relationships among social forces that can then be used to explain the existence, meaning, and purpose of the police and the criminal justice system. The following is an example of this: rising crime rates produce citizen demands for more police, harsher penalties for criminals, larger and more sophisticated prisons.

These self-evaluations are generally holistic in nature, and they invariably concentrate on the process of criminal justice in terms of substantive and procedural law, the procedure for administering the law, and the impact or causal relationship between the system and society. Foremost in this perspective is a concern with the question *what*—what

3

are the components of the system and what are they doing? But this concern tends to ignore the question *why*—why are there such existing components to the criminal justice system and why do they respond to society in the way that they do?

It is the purpose of this book to seek out answers to the question *why* —why do we have a police force and a criminal justice system in America and what are the true sociological ends being served by them; or better still, to what ends are they being asked to serve? We may discover that what the police are expected to accomplish is more important for society than their actual performance. In any event, trying to answer the question *why* should be helpful in gaining a greater understanding of the police role in American society.

SOCIAL ORDER

At the outset, let it be said that the primary function of the police is not crime fighting, but that of attempting to maintain social order. This is implied by the notion of law and order; the emphasis in the latter case is placed on those who would break the law, and in the former case emphasis is on those who would protect it. This is not at all a subtle distinction, but it generally passes unrecognized by the police and the public.

Law and order in its commonplace sense has come to be understood as the mandate of the police to enforce the laws of society in the face of those citizens who would break it. Implicit in this mandate is the assumption that there are those individuals who want to break the law, and indeed they are probably unable to prevent themselves from doing so. Consequently, the police are needed to protect society from those rogues who by their nature do not have the will to abide by the civility of a society that is governed by a system of laws. If rogues accept any law, it is likely to be the "law of the jungle."

Also, the law and order theme tends to attribute a certain purity to the law in and of itself. The law we speak of is not the Ten Commandments handed down by God, but rather the laws that were formed and shaped by mortals to be used in a secular world of egos and self-interest. By the same token, this theme would also have us believe that the police are impersonal functionaries, just doing their jobs, carrying out the will of the majority, if not society overall. Of course, we know that both these views are entirely unrealistic.

Social order advances on us from another perspective. Social order exists through the maintenance of the conditions of society that promote stability and reaffirm traditional values that support it. Implicit in this statement is the assumption that the people of society want to abide by the law as it reflects a desire for stability, and to be sure they not only desire stability, but are willing to act accordingly to ensure its presence. Therefore, in this social context, there is no need for a police body; a coercive force to make people abide by the law. The people would do it willingly because they recognize that it serves their interest for social order. And, make no mistake about it, police power in the first instance is not solely directed at the criminals of society, but rather at society overall. This is what the law and order theme calls for because it is not known at the outset which individuals will break the law.

Under the social order aegis, purity cannot automatically be attributed to the law. The law is understood to be just one means by which society attempts to maintain social order. Consequently, the law is not to be taken as an end in itself. In a similar manner, the police would not be perceived as social managers, if indeed there would even be such a body as the police. The idea that a specified group of individuals should be given the responsibility for keeping order in society would be innocuous to the premise that people are essentially willing to abide by the rules and norms of the social system as a means of ensuring their stability.

But of course, the negative attitude does prevail. Socially we generally believe that people are unable to maintain order in society without social managers, and the history of humankind would seem to bear this out. Yet the idea that people should, and can, maintain social order without the need of a police force is nevertheless a long-standing social ideal. Philosophers during the Age of Enlightenment gave much support to the idea that people were basically good and, given the proper social environment, could maintain a free, compassionate society. However the societies that those philosophers dreamed about has not reached fruition in our time.

The point being made here is that basically our society, and this seems to be true of all Western societies, has adopted the posture that people are basically bad or prone to be so. Or to put it in the context of Emile Durkheim's notion of *homo duplex*, people by their very natures are unable to entirely control themselves. It is then up to society, its collective conscience, to be the controlling force for the individual. That is why, the thinking goes, people form societies and submit themselves to its social controls.

Our Judaeo-Christian religion also takes this posture with its idea of *original sin* and the need for God's laws, His Commandments, to guide the behavior of its believers. There is even a suggestion of Christianity's lack of faith in the good character of people indicated by the need of religion to try to regulate the secular life of its believers with the explicit threat of hell waiting for them after death if they do not live a good life on earth. Even more threatening is God's reminder that a flood was once used to cleanse the earth of the ill-fated lifestyles of humankind, but it will be *the fire next time* if we fall to such ruinous, morally corrupting ways again. Remember *Sodom* and *Gomorrah.*

Our society prides itself on the fact that it is based on a system of laws and not the power of men. We appeal to objectivity in our political institutions and the general decision making for society. The Constitution of the United States and the Supreme Court stand as symbols to our faith in the impersonal administration of justice and the maintenance of law and order in society. But this cultural attitude suggests that if people were left to their own subjective devices, injustice and disorder are likely to result.

While the negative attitude about human nature doth prevail in our society, this does not mean that more positive attitudes are without some influence. In fact, in some respects the American political scene reflects both sides of the human character issue. Conservative politicians are more likely to see people in the negative attitude already mentioned, and liberals tend to take the more positive side. The most interesting fact about this is that politicians are the ones who make the laws that the police are asked to enforce and the public abide by. But with both sides of this character issue influencing legislation, it makes for contradictory, often ambiguous law.

For the above mentioned reasons, conservative politicians are more likely to support the police rather than not, while the matter is the opposite for the liberals. But what makes this situation an even more muddled affair for society is that conservative minded individuals are the ones who seem to be most interested in reaffirming traditions, and liberals seem to be the ones who are forever tinkering with them. As a consequence, it appears as though the conservative individuals are the people who care most about the social order, as we have been discussing it, than, say, the more liberal minded folk. However the distinction can be cleared up by understanding that what concerns conservatives is stability in society more than the process of social order. The two are not necessarily compatible, and as social forces they may well be in conflict.

As the police take a posture for law and order, their position is clearly a conservative one. They see the public as potential lawbreakers, a source for disrupting social order. In this sense the police, perhaps inadvertently, set themselves against the public to be served, and in effect deny the public the right to be responsible for social order. By tradition and law, the police believe that the maintenance of social order is their responsibility, for they perceive themselves as having the training, the willingness, the organization, the weaponry, and the essential power to do so. Of course the police, like the public, do mistake the maintenance of law and order for the maintenance of social order. For this reason, a greater distinction needs to be made in what is the process of social order because the posture taken by the police puts them in conflict with society's attempts, as reflected in the individual, to maintain social order.

Society has mistakenly delegated to the police the responsibility for maintaining social order. It is a mistake because this is a process that can only be carried out by individual members of society acting collectively for their common good. The maintenance of social order cannot be allocated to a band of individuals who, by the nature of the task assigned to them, must separate themselves from other members of society. If social order comes about because of feelings of social solidarity among the group's members, then the police as a separate social entity unto themselves, act against the enhancement of social solidarity. For they become law or rule enforcers, individuals who in effect see themselves above the law. The law is made for those who might break it, not for those who are dedicated to enforce it. This is to say that the law is but a justification for the actions of the law enforcers, and in this way the law serves the police, as a special interest group, much more than society.

It is only the people, and not the police, who can maintain social order because it serves the people's interest and not the interest of the police. If there were true social order in society there would be no need for the police. The public, as an ongoing general habit, would abide by the rules, the regulations, the laws, the norms of society. This being the case, there would be little or nothing for the police, as we understand them today, to do. The presence of lawbreakers justifies the presence of the police. The police exist because of the presence of social disorder.

One could extend this premise to the conclusion that the police, for their own survival, must inevitably work against social order, but this would be ever so hard to specifically determine as a function of the police overall. Nevertheless, it can be stated that the police, by their very presence in society, must produce tension between themselves and the people, regardless of the amount of lawbreaking that goes on. Further, and this point is even more speculative, it may be that the police are social inspirators. They inspire both good and bad in people; good for the obvious reason of the stability they are believed to bring to society, and bad to justify their existence. And there may well be a much larger sociological issue at work in this context, for Durkheim said that societies have a need for the criminal. It gives society the chance to demonstrate to the people its capability of administering punishment.

Social order is likely to be made more maintainable by adherence to the law, as the law reflects customs and social norms. But this is not the same as saying that the laws have to be enforced over the populace by an armed constabulary. In fact, the situation suggests that laws that have to be enforced over the people are not necessarily laws that the people in a collective group will find acceptable. In other words, the laws may not reflect the general customs and norms of the people who are asked to abide by them. This fact depicts the awkwardness of our political sense of democracy, where laws are not truly made collectively by the people who must live by them, but are made by separate bodies known as legislatures.

These lawmakers, while seemingly owing their offices to the faith invested in them by electoral constituencies, do not necessarily feel obligated to make law and policy that specifically serves their constituents' interests. Certainly, the opposite is true. Once a politician takes office, his view of society is different than the people who put him there. The politician is likely to see himself or herself as part of the power structure of society rather than being accountable to it. Like the police, they make laws to regulate society and not themselves. Too, legislators are very influenced by lobbyists, more so than they are by their constituents because lobbyists offer them campaign dollars and other quiet amenities.

This is to say that the laws from our separate bodies known as legislatures are more likely to serve special interests rather than society as a whole; hence, politicians tend to make policy and laws that use the people more than serve them. Perhaps one reason the police are needed, in a very elemental sense, is to enforce laws that the public at large, in many cases, cannot accept as basically being in their interest.

Of course, the American society is extraordinarily polygloted, being politically and culturally stratified along racial, ethnic, color, class, money, and religious lines. At the same time, our society is largely run by a white, Anglo-Saxon, Protestant (WASP) cultural heritage. It is this group that holds the economic and political reins of power today. Consequently, the laws mandated by our legislatures are likely to reflect their sense of customs and their sense of norms. And frankly, the laws are likely to serve their interest in the first instance. This means that for the various social groups that are further from the social center, that is, those whose social habits are less compatible with the WASP's sense of customs and norms, the laws of our society will be less indicative of the values that govern their lifestyles.

It can probably be said with some accuracy that police enforcement of the laws will grow with intensity as the groups under enforcement are socially and culturally situated further and further from the social center, and again this would have nothing to do with the amount of lawbreaking involved. The law, by its nature, would be less suitable to the lifestyle of those groups and less compatible with their lesser commitments to WASP values.

Because of the extreme nature of our socially stratified system, social order would be difficult to maintain in any event. To be sure, the most substantive readings of the situation suggest that a rigid form of social order, broadly unified across all groups, is probably impossible. Therefore, what has resulted is the emergence of subcultural enclaves based on racial, ethnic, or religious ties, to the exclusion of other groups, and there is a kind of limited ethnocentric order that is maintained among the participants of the various enclaves. However, this has committed our society to a form of internecine struggle for political power and economic opportunity. The successes of some groups, versus the failures of others, can be seen in the manner in which some are more favored by the laws and some are favored less. The police have much to say about this process.

This internecine struggle will tend to lessen the chances of the citizenry to have a broad based feeling of solidarity among them, and by the same token it gives rise to a strong need for an enforcement arm in society that will make less favored groups conform to the ways of the more favored groups.

It is probably true to say that our culture overly stresses behavior as the initial starting point for the maintenance of social order. That is the basis for our type of system of laws. They are directed at controlling people's behavior, behavior not so much for the self, but behavior directed towards others. While outward behavior does example the presence of social order or disorder, the starting point for either does not actually lie with this manner of human expression. Most human behavior is probably defined and thought out ahead of time, and much of it comes from the prescribed roles that result from our socialization. This is not to ignore spontaneous responses to immediate stimuli from the environment, but still most behavior is predictable based upon learned beliefs and values that have shaped the person emotionally. In speaking of the maintenance of social order, a person's outward behavior is probably less important than his belief and value systems.

In attempting to maintain social order, one's attitudes towards right and wrong are more important than the commission of acts that are considered right or the commission of acts that are considered wrong. This is the case because the starting point for either group of actions is likely to be based upon one's sense of morality and ethics. This fact poses a difficult problem for a society that tries to live by the rule of law, because as the old adage makes clear, it is impossible to legislate morality.

As America has placed its faith for social order in laws, the system has given up, in a meaningful sense, the right to have a society that relies on a certain fundamental morality, for such a basis would have to reside within the populace at large and not outside of it as our system of laws would suggest. Instead of having a basic fundamental morality, a basic understanding for all society's members of what is right and wrong in a behavioral and philosophical sense, we have given to the people a police force. It is the police who are being asked to be the conscience of society because we do not put credence in the individual's ability to control his actions, or his ability to prevent himself from breaking the law.

However, it is individual willpower and conscience that must be the basis for a true system of social order simply because of the logistics of the problem involved. Unless there is going to be one police officer for each individual, or each household, there would never be enough police officers to constitute a true supernumerary and superordinate conscience for society. The preponderance of the numbers needed would make the society a true police state in every sense of the term and would still not accomplish what is intended. But the police, and the criminal justice system overall, is in its function being called upon to be the arbitrator of societal morality.

Police power, in our society, is being substituted for individual willpower, and in the process society is taking the view that the individual is morally incapable of regulating his own behavior for the good of the social system and for the good of himself. This is a demeaning description of human nature. This requires, in a manner of speaking, that an individual accept the notion that he is weak of character, if not a morally corrupting force with respect to his participation as a member of the collective will and consciousness. It also gives to the police the image of being a morally inspiring force. As the police are understood to carry out the law, this further lends credence to the idea of the inherent morality of the law over the inherent immorality of the individual.

A society that is governed by laws must inevitably stress the starting point for its concept of social order on collective action rather than the individual will. Our society takes a fundamental position regardless of its political and cultural propaganda, that the system is more important than the individual, and that a purpose of society is to make the individual bend and submit to the collective will. If there is to be a choice between the individual conscience and the collective conscience, then individual conscience must be sacrificed. Whereas the police may function as society's conscience, in matters of choice between the police and the public to be served, it is the police who are likely to get the better of it than the public.

Even though our society stresses the importance of itself over its individual members, this in no way changes the fact that social order bespeaks, in the first instance of individuals freely cooperating within a collective unit, rather than a situation of individuals being coerced to cooperate by social managers and the power of law enforcement. Social order should not be motivated by fear, threat of arrest, incarceration, and ostracization from society. Without cooperation freely given, that cooperation is surely suspect.

The fact that our society so outlandishly preaches the ideology of freedom, while in effect the society operates under a system of coercive laws, makes the situation even more innocuous. It allows the simple explanation that police action is for maintaining order which accounts for the freedom that our society supposedly offers to its citizens. But there seems to be little understanding that the presence of a system of laws, whose specific purpose is that of governing the behavior of citizens, suggests that freedom, as behavior freely exercised, is lacking.

A society that maintains itself by a system of laws is seemingly unaware that social order can only be maintained by individuals freely cooperating with one another. It is the only way they can really believe that the order being maintained is for their own good. It is a decision each person makes for himself on the basis of his values and his morality. He cooperates because he feels morally compelled to do so and because he feels he has an obligation to cooperate with other members of the society. In this instance, the individual becomes his own social manager.

Therefore, the pressure to conform is from an internal source rather than an external one, like that of the police. When the pressure to conform is external in source and nature, the individual can always perceive of it as being applied against his will, no matter how legitimate the authority or righteous the purpose. It is the external origins of the pressure to conform that delimits its effectiveness. As police are generally the source for this external pressure, it could be said that the police presence in society probably tends to delimit social conformity to those laws and standards they represent.

One might ask, if the police presence is so alien to the proper maintenance of social order, why have we cultivated their presence in society? To begin with, the question assumes that it is our society's intention to have a system of social order as I have been discussing it here, when indeed that may not be the case. Indeed, the fact that we have a police force to maintain order in society suggests otherwise. Further, we know that our society lauds itself on the ideals of freedom and equality that is supposedly offered to all individuals regardless of social differences. Yet, we also know this is not the reality of the way the system operates.

Our society is built on favoritism of some groups over others. If ours is a free society, then some groups are freer than others. The whites are favored over the blacks, the Hispanics, Indians, and other minorities. The WASPS are favored over the Catholics and the Jews; urban dwellers over rural dwellers. The normal, healthy person is favored over the handicapped person, and on and on it goes. Our society is built on prejudice and discrimination. This alone should tell us that a broad system of social solidarity is not sought, and therefore is likely unobtainable in our society. Given this picture of our society, the presence of the police, in the context that I have been describing them, makes much better sense.

As it was pointed out earlier, the laws, and of consequence the police, serve the dominant cultural interest of our society; which is to say, they serve the powerful vested interests of our social system. As our society is also invested with a capitalist ideology of profit, self-interest, and enterpreneurial values, contest and struggle for personal gain is a basic cultural motif. Individuals struggle for profit and power and so do the many different social groups. The police may well be an expression of one group's attempt to gain, maintain, and control the basic power sources of society. If this is not thoroughly true, at least it offers some explanation of the contradictory nature of the police with respect to this society's quest for an authentic system of social order.

SOCIAL EVOLUTION

The American society today does not attempt to maintain a system of social order that is based upon the moral judgments of the individual. Indeed, the general consensus would very likely be that such a social process is an idealistic, utopian view. Such disclaimers are unfortunate because it makes our dependency on the police and their mandate of maintaining law and order even more inevitable in the present societal context, and it furthers the belief that society as we understand it is not practical without law enforcement. Happily, a full discussion of this belief is probably more suited to the pursuits of philosophers than sociologists, and therefore it will not be entertained here.

At the same time, it is pertinent to this discussion to consider how American society came to be dependent upon the police and their law and order function. The response to this is to be found in the evolution of Western societies over the past few hundred years; which is to say the transition period of Western societies from pre–modern to modern times.

Social scientists are in general agreement with the fact that the modern era was ushered to the forefront in Western societies by the breakdown of the traditional system of authority that had existed under the feudal monarchs of Europe for many centuries. That system of authority rested on the power of the monarch in the secular world, supported by the power of the church in the spiritual world. The feudal society was a class society in the extreme, and one's class was determined by birth. This fact determined one's status in society for life; that is to say, it generally defined one's social behavior and lifestyle as well. "As did my father, so do I."

While the classes, the monarchical family, the lords and nobles (which included the clergy), and the serfs or peasants were kept socially separated, they were held together in a common bond by a sense of obligation each group had to the other. The church gave its blessing to this social arrangement and the class system was thereby thought to be designated by God. To break class ranks was to break the personal covenant every Christian had with God. This gave to the church enormous power over the individual behaviors of the people.

The church's power was further enhanced by a fundamental belief that was held by all classes, that the world was infested with satanic evil. It was a fallen angel, Satan, who was trying to steal their souls while the church was trying to protect them. There was an ongoing battle between good and evil; the devil on one side and God on the other. As the church spoke for God, the best way to defend oneself from this satanic evil was to be a good Christian and abide by church law. Church law was basically irrational and therefore its acceptance was based not on logic, but rather on faith and blind belief. This meant that each individual had to assume his responsibility for his faith and his beliefs. It was not only that the church would hold him accountable to this, but consistent with each person's personal covenant with God, the individual had to hold himself accountable.

While the monarch, with help from the nobles and lords, ruled in the secular world, this manner of rule was also decidedly irrational. That is to say, the power was not based on reasoning social premises that were essentially established by a system of rational laws, but instead it was mainly determined by the idea of *noblesse oblige,* the obligation of rank that was inferred by a "blue blood" birth. For those of this class, and the serfs who gave respect to it, their acceptance of this system was as much a matter of faith as it was the reigning belief in the ever-present devil as a socially subverting evil force. The monarch, his nobles and lords were treated like little gods in the secular world.

Each class was expected to look after its obligations to the others and to itself. The failing of individual members was seen as a failing of the class as a whole. Therefore, members of the same class took particular care to see that their fellow members adhered to their obligation as they did not want a negative reflection upon them. This made the spirit of solidarity and camaraderie rather strong, for individuals did see themselves as their *brother's keeper.*

Among the commoners, the "red bloods," the family in traditional society was strong, and it had to be, for there were no welfare agencies to look after the health and well-being of individual societal members. One's social security came from a strong family unit that was obligated to look after its own in sickness, health, and old age. And, the internal mechanisms of the family were also fitted around the obligations of each member to the unit as a whole. The family as a unit was understood to be more important than its individual members, and one carried out his duties with that always in mind. To be ostracized by one's family was to be cut off socially and set adrift, to be made anonymous and without the security that only the family could provide. The ostracized person became a pariah within his own community, and he was also labelled a malignant social entity.

The family was seen as belonging to society more than belonging to its individual members. It was the family which bound the individual members to the community. One's actions as a member of a family would ultimately be reflected upon the community, and the community was understood to be more important than any one individual family. Each family held its obligations to the community in the highest esteem because in many respects it was the community which made family possible.

Unity within the community was based upon cooperation among all its members. The traditional community did not have a strict division of labor system. The necessary tasks needed to maintain the whole community were done by the people acting as one main group. Fighting the ravages of nature or humankind was dealt with as a collective front. These were agrarian communities. Each family maintained its farm land, but when individual farmers needed help other members of the community would support him. Help was given willingly and freely because people recognized that they were all dependent on each other for basic survival.

Cooperation was more easily obtained because people knew one another on a personal, one-to-one basis, and by and large they had the same values and participated in the same institutional settings. They were socially alike in almost every way within their particular class. There was a strong common identity, and to protect and help one's neighbor was done as much for oneself as it was done for the other person.

To this sense of community the church offered a strong set of edicts on morality and ethics of proper behavior and the need to respect and cooperate with one's neighbor. It was God who called upon the people of the community to live as brethren, and any aspersions upon this social proclamation was to cast aspersions upon the will of God. That could mean excommunication from the church which would not only affect the person in this life, but emphatically it would affect him after death. The chances of life ever after in the bosom of God would be threatened.

At the same time, the monarch, and nobles and lords also gave their support and blessing to a cooperating peasant community because their basic sustenance was dependent upon it. The blue bloods did not work in the common sense of tilling the soil and harvesting its rewards. That was the job of the peasants who usually did not own the land that they worked on, but rather it was owned by one or another blue blood and they actually worked the land for them, each receiving a share of the harvest. Hence the entire feudal economy ran on the backs of the peasants, the serfs. To be sure, the peasants even formed the basis for the monarch's armies. There were no standing, professional armies in those days, as there was also no police force in any sense that we understand it today. The people had to look after themselves, provide their own protection.

The feudal society existed in Europe for many hundreds of years, and during its better epochs it was quite strong and stable. When the system did begin to weaken, it was not so much due to the peasants (the overwhelming majority of the population), but due more to the power struggles that ensued for many generations among the blue bloods. This is not to say that the peasants did not have reasons to want to change the feudal society. They may have had a strong sense of community and fellow-feeling among themselves, but at the same time they were wretchedly poor most of the time and greatly abused by the lords and nobles. Nevertheless, they bided their time and made do the best they could.

But in the final analysis, it was the Age of Reason, the Enlightenment, that brough an end to feudalism. The Enlightenment movement in Europe called for greater egalitarianism and a breakdown of the old class structures that kept political power in the hands of the blue bloods. Democratic institutions were needed that would allow all the people, including the peasants, to share in the uses of political power. The faith and the belief in the church, as a source for the traditional systems of authority, were thought to be inadequate for the new kind of polity that was being called for. Society should have a more secular basis for its operations and less of a spiritual one. The church was too concerned with life after death and not enough concerned with the life people were required to live on earth.

As new institutions of authority based on constitutional governments and a system of laws that were to be administered through a judiciary process arose, a novel social philosophy emerged. In part it stated that freedom was the right of all individuals, and this right was to be guaranteed by society's laws. Everyone was to be treated equally and fairly before the law, to ensure the fact that individual rights would not be abridged. One would no longer have to depend on religious faith and fellow-feeling, camaraderie and social interdependence, as a basis for one's commitment to the community, to society. One only had to show respect for the law, and this would suffice. But in truth, the people were not only being asked to respect the law. They were also being asked to put their sense of religious faith and moral righteousness in the law.

Over a period of time, Western peoples came to rely upon the laws of their societies to give them the reasons, the purpose, the inspiration for the character of their social behavior. Public performance became very much a matter of what the law required. The United States of America was in the forefront of this movement due to its early development of a constitutional form of government.

Society's system of laws was raised to a higher status than the people. Whereas people make laws, and it is believed that the laws should serve people, in fact under the present social philosophy, the written, rational laws of social conduct actually cause the people to serve them. When there are doubts, as to the meaning of the law when matched to individual behavior, the law tends to be favored over the individual. This is particularly true if the behavior is considered criminal.

A new system of social organization also arose to administer the laws of society. The modern bureaucratic organization emerged, which was very well suited for its purposes. Bureaucracy encouraged notions of abstract authority as represented by rational laws and governmental constitutions, and courtroom judicial processes. In the past, authority had been represented by people, the community, the society. But in the new era, authority had come to be inhuman and abstract. It was an idea, not a concrete reality. It was a means, not an end.

This meant that politics, the basis for group, societal action also came to be represented in abstract ideas. Politics and its ensuing decision-making became the result of ideologies and not conscience, and the entire process of political decision-making inevitably moved towards a depersonalized posture. Political behavior and the average social behavior were being dictated by the same abstract quality.

The new polity of this new philosophy, following the lead of the Enlightenment philosophers, called for everyone of proper mature age to participate in the politics of society, which meant that they were expected to share in the ideological process of politics. The more people became

involved the more they found themselves committed to the depersonaliza-
tion of the process. And it was something that people could not readily
back away from because they were made to feel that decision-making
under this form of policy was dependent upon a consensus reached among
societal members before political action could be taken. This made
people even more dependent upon the nature of the political process, and
less upon themselves and each other.

Under the emerging political aegis, the people of society were recognized as political constituencies, who in effect were in themselves bereft
of political power. That power came to rest in the political process which
culminated in the exercise of government. In traditional society, this fact
of life was the province of one's community, and it was the people in their
communities who made decisions that directly affected their lives. But
now that process was indirect at best, and as a practical matter, in effect,
the process was totally absent from the judgments of nongovernmental
citizens.

These new social processes were forming a basis and delivering a
philosophy that made it less likely that people would be willing to act
as a community of brethren who did indeed need to depend upon
one another, cooperate with one another, for their own survival's sake.
And this was made even more clear by the values proliferating in
society as a consequence of the coming of capitalist economies.

Under capitalism, the profit motive governed the economy. The social
world became a world that was viewed as an arena for the games of competition. It was a world that bespoke of the situation; it is *me* against
them. It was a world of personal gain at the expense of others. In fact,
it may be necessary to exploit others for one's own personal gain, and this
was not to be seen as unfair. The ideals of the rugged individualist were
also entwined in the new values of capitalism. Success produced the best
for those who could individually stand up to the rigors of tough competition. If you did not beat your brethren in a fair, competitive fight for
profit, then it was likely that he would end up beating you. It was "dog
eat dog" if one wanted to get ahead.

The spirit of personal gain had overtaken the need for community
spirit. Serve yourself first and then it was permissible to see what, if
anything, could be done for the community as a whole. Indeed it was
that the community in itself had become nothing but a crucible to be used
in the race for success, wealth, and achievement. Community spirit was to
be manipulated for personal advantage, which also meant that one's
ability to use others, in the most pejorative sense, for one's own ends and
personal success, was a quality that was to be socially praised and
admired.

With society's individual members in the modern era now more than ever concerned about their individual interests and gain, diversity became commonplace to the system. People chose their values on the basis of how well it would serve their needs and interests. If values could help one become a success, then they were adopted; if not, they were likely to be rejected. There was no common morality in a practical sense. Morality was to serve particular interests, whoever's interest was involved. The church could be of no help because that institution was, in time, relegated to the Sunday schooling of the masses. Church edict and law was something to talk about, but it was not necessarily something one adhered to in his everyday life. Imagine if people actually believed that all humans were brethren, we would be less inclined to take advantage of each other and to exploit one another.

Gone also was the commonality of the workplace. Under the feudal economy, most people were farmers. There was a commonality in their endeavors to obtain and maintain a flow of sustenance. But in the modern world, there were literally thousands of different workplaces, many of them competing against each other, many of them emphasizing the worker's economic life chances differently. This also had much to say about the fact that people were participating in many different institutions, and not all the people were participating in the same ones. For instance, where Catholicism had been the philosophy of the church during the feudal times, there are many different religions being practiced in the modern world, and the diversity is a source for the many different bases for morality and individual social values.

Still other factors further exacerbated the lack of community spirit and sense of togetherness of the people in the modern world. Populations had grown tremendously due to medical advances. These populations, totalling in the millions, made up communities in the hundreds of thousands, whereas feudal communities had been small, small enough for the people to know one another, formulate personal relationships on a one-to-one basis. But with numbers of people in the community totalling in the hundreds of thousands, it was physically impossible for all the people to get to know each other.

The growth of populations in the modern era has largely occurred in urban centers that surround cities. The cities held the commerce, the jobs, the opportunities. Prior to the urbanization of the American society, most of the people lived in small rural areas, but as the society became more industrialized it became more dependent upon the urban community with its network of communications, transportation systems, labor, and markets all tied together. When it became clear that the future of the American economy resided in the cities, young people from the rural areas began to migrate to the cities, along with many other displeased and displaced workers, and this sought to break the ties of the old family networks and the camaraderie of friendships that had existed in these rural areas which had helped to hold these smaller communities together. Once people migrated to the cities they tended not to return to the rural districts. The old rural types of traditional communities were being left behind in favor of city living, an urban style of life.

Modern city life emerged without the traditions of rural agrarian life. City life had emerged from the marketplace. In its beginning it had been a place where people could come and gather to do trading and buying of produce. Its tradition was that of entrepreneurial endeavors founded on capitalist values of profit-making. As the cities developed more fully, these values became the basis for community life and neighborly relations. The unrelenting diveristy of it, the competition, the striving for personal gain in place of a collective spirit produced a social attitude of strangers living amongst the crowd, strangers trying very hard to remain impersonal and unrevealing to others who surrounded them.

During the emergence of the modern era, American society was also being greatly influenced by these social turns of events, but unlike other Western European societies, Americans were also confronted with the fatigue, passion, and animosities of race relations between blacks and whites in society. This was another reason that prevented a traditional social coalescence for Americans. Blacks were to be kept specifically away from their "white betters" and kept socially bordered up in ghetto environments; while at the same time their labor power was to be used in factories and white homes to make life easier for the whites. This was a blatant, ongoing denigration of America's black citizens. In a manner of speaking, the blacks along with other ethnic minorities of color and Hispanic backgrounds had come to assume the status that once had been alloted to the lowly serfs and peasants of the feudal era. They were to rest on the bottom of the social structure, to be the pillars on which the upper strata of the system would rest. Being exploited and taken advantage of was their given lot in life.

We began this section with the intention of trying to get a better understanding as to why the American society, and Western societies in general, have become dependent upon the police as the chief tool for attempting to maintain social order. We can see now that the institutions of pre-modern society that performed in the role were denuded and deemphasized by the transitional forces that ushered in the modern era. For instance, urbanization drained the small rural communities that had been the basis for the social life in pre-modern society, and it forced a build-up of massive populations in a very small geographical area. The populations of the cities had come to live together not out of an interest in caring and sharing among one another, but they had come to live in the same environment as a result of individual desires for economic and social gain. Rather than feeling camaraderie for one another, people were more likely to see and feel themselves being in a face-off with competitors. This gave to the cities a natural tension between the people. There was, and still is, an inherent propensity in urban life of struggling to best, and be better than your neighbor.

Add to this the normal stratification that is found in any society, then one could easily conclude that modern urban living is truly a rat race which is ensconced in a human pressure cooker. And the lifestyle of the majority of Americans today is decidedly urban in character.

City life is possessed of diversity and overflowing with disparate groups, socially, politically, ethnically, racially, religiously, and culturally. American society as a whole is fashioned in the same way. Given this fact, Americans find themselves generally bereft of a unifying morality that would bind them all to consistent judgments of what is right and what is wrong. They are burdened with diverse systems of values, and overall they lack a true sense of traditional community spirit. It should come as no surprise then that the American people as individuals have been unable to manage and maintain on their own volition a concerted program of social order.

From this perspective, it would seem that some social instrument is needed to maintain at least a semblance of social order if the citizenry cannot do it for themselves. Therefore, our society, and all modern societies, have handed this responsibility over to a system of rational laws and law enforcement managers. It is the nation's police force that has come to fill the vacuum once occupied by society's individual members. But, in doing this we may have given up a fundamental responsibility that is, in effect, non-transferable. The individual will cannot be delegated to any subsidiary authority, even though we may collectively acquiesce to that authority. Without our individual, personal efforts in the maintenance of social order, a reliance upon our subjective conscience, then social order in the traditional context may not be possible.

Having reached this conclusion, as tentative as it may be, it leads us to another set of interesting, if vexing questions. If, in the final analysis, the police are unable to maintain social order, then what essential purpose are they serving in society today? Why have we given them such enormous power over our lives? And why have we given them the right to execute citizens in the performance of their duties? Why do we both praise and condemn the police on a regular basis? And lastly, why do we have such a latent fear of the presence of police power in our society?

Through the remainder of this book, I will attempt to develop answers to these and many other questions. But even at this junction in the book, it should come as no surprise that already you can hear them, the police, knocking.

2

MAINTAINING THE STATUS QUO

America as a society describes itself as a democratic nation; this is to say, a system where essential political power remains in the hands of the people. Whether the American people actually have such power, or rather that the power is in the hands of certain elite groups, is a debatable subject. Nevertheless, the American political system, the nation's polity, and let us call it democratic for the sake of clarity, is reputed to be based on a consensus decision-making model. Consensus model may be defined as the process by which individuals and groups work out their differences amicably as a basis for political decision-making. Central to the process is the willingness of participants to seek and reach agreement and an understanding amidst their differences that is acceptable to all. This requires making divergent points of view compatible by ideationally molding them into new patterns that emphasize their likeness rather than their differences. Theoretically, in this process, the will of the majority prevails in the end.

However, experience has shown us that it is quite difficult for a society to maintain a consensus model of politics. This is particularly true in societies like America where there are enormous populations, in the millions, spread out over a very wide geographical area. The larger the population, the greater the likelihood of divergent political views among the people and the wide expanse of geography tends to encourage regionalism, in the socio-cultural sense. Plus, in the modern world, due to our dependency upon machines the social scene tends to be constantly buffeted by technological change that directly influences the lives of the citizenry, and these changes do not impact on all citizens in a similar manner. Consequently, individual citizens and groups tend to personalize

22

public decision-making on the basis of how it will serve their interests, their chances for being productive, meaningful, successful, and their ultimate quest for basic sustenance.

The consensus model tends to serve most of those individuals who can best influence the process through persuasion, coercion, and intimidation of others who disagree with them. Political power and vested interest are the dominating factors in the process at the outset, and therefore free discussion is inhibited as a fact of the process itself. Decisions are not then, necessarily, freely made, but more to the truth they are induced by representatives of the centers of power and influence.

But what makes the maintenance of the consensus model even more difficult is the fact that in order for it to attempt operations, much less to actually work effectively, it is necessary that the participants be philosophically and ideologically of a like mind. There must be some common basis among the participants at the outset that would make a consensus possible. A staunch capitalist and a staunch socialist are not likely to have much to agree upon in matters of social policy. Therefore democratic societies attempt to maintain a core philosophy and ideology that the majority of its people can agree with as a starting point for negotiations that can lead to a consensus for political decision-making.

At the same time, democratic societies bespeak of their citizenry as being free. Citizens have the right of freedom of choice, which is to say that the people are told that they do not have to obligate themselves to a particular philosophy or ideology, except in the broadest sense of adhering to democratic principles. This means that a democratic society, by its nature, creates an inordinate strain within its political process by needing a basic political credo on the one hand, but also needing to disqualify it on the other hand. If nothing else, it creates confusion and muddledness in the consensus process.

Add to this the ideology of the rugged individualist, and the other values of a capitalist mentality, one can readily realize that there is great encouragement for Americans not to strictly adhere to one basic political credo for society as a whole. Moreover, racial prejudice and discrimination has forced colored, ethnic minorities to live socially in subcultures and as marginal groups to the social mainstream. This has caused them not only to question the nation's basic political belief, but it has put them in a position of contesting it for their own survival's sake.

Given this character of the American social reality, it is extremely important to the system to maintain its central philosophical and ideological core if there is to be any possibility for the society to affect even the pretense of operating on a political consensus model of decision-making. In this matter, image may be more important than substance.

This seems to be borne out by the fact that democratic societies, and America in the extreme sense, do tend to be obsessed with the desire to defend and protect its core values.

The elements of America's essential philosophy and ideology are to be found in her political and economic traditions by and large. We have already spoken of them—those values that are concomitant with a capitalist social orientation and those beliefs that bespeak of societies governed by rational constitutions and laws rather than by the fiat of individual persons. Protecting these core elements from social erosion and social change has come to be the basis for our understanding of the notorious idea that society needs to maintain the *status quo*. The core traditions represent the American mainstream. They further represent the ideology of America's central political authority and that ideology is expressed through government policies which supposedly represent the nation as a whole. As a consequence, it has been left to government and its agents to be the chief instruments for protecting the status quo.

What is it that government and its agents are specifically protecting for society? Government is to protect our sacred traditions that make democracy possible. And who is government to protect these values from? Excluding foreign social forces, government protection opposes those individuals and groups of Americans who wish to act counter to the sacred traditions that represent the mainstream of society. For example, in the 1960s when black Americans were protesting against the prejudice and discrimination they had long endured, at the outset they were treated as a subversive social element.

At the same time, individuals and groups that are situated at society's social center are not likely to feel the need to question the system's basic philosophy because they tend to live by the edicts of the sacred traditions and because they benefit most from its rewards. The government and its agents have a propensity to embrace them. The group that most symbolizes the social center is the white middle class. But among those groups who are not situated at the social center, like the colored, ethnic minorities, there is the tendency of the government and its agents to suspiciously and benignly tolerate them.

Needless to say, in order to maintain a basis for political consensus, the American society must be constantly concerned with any and all aspects of the system that might affect the status quo. Therefore, those individuals and groups of the social periphery, who question the status quo, are held in deep suspicion by members of the social center and in particular by the police. Fringe groups are not to be allowed to endanger the status quo.

For the reasons just mentioned, our government finds it necessary to keep a close watch over its citizens. It is the police on the streets who accomplish this through a policing network that covers the country, and in effect allows the government, on a day-to-day basis to penetrate the citizens' daily lives.[1] It is for this reason that America can be described as a policed society.[2] This is to say that the American society has a professional corps of police officers stationed throughout civilian communities, whose express purpose is that of policing the citizens. They exist as an arm of government, and they have been given the authority and physical potential to exercise violent supervision over the citizenry.

To be sure, the individual police officers are not instructed in the facts of the matter as related here. The police see themselves as maintaining law and order and thereby stability in society, but for all practical purposes stability is equated with the maintenance of the status quo. This results because maintaining the status quo is understood to come about through resistance to social erosion and social change. For the police to maintain stability is therefore for the police to work for the maintenance of the status quo.

Of course, as the police work for the maintenance of the status quo they must inevitably give support to the ranking system, the stratification network of society. Therefore, they give protection to the vested interests of those who hold political power and positions of influence. Police actions tend to favor certain individuals and groups over others which is a natural outgrowth of their role in a democratic society. The police are then a major feature of this nation's polity, irrespective of criminal behavior. Our society has had a definite need for the police ever since it declared itself a nation to be governed by democratic principles.

THE FEAR OF DECENTRALIZED GOVERNANCE

Contrary to what most Americans believe, today the police are not basically constituted to serve the interests of criminal law enforcement. They are used to surveying and scrutinizing all citizens—not just the potentially bad ones—as a fact of our democratic process. To stimulate our thinking along this course, we should recall the excesses of law enforcement during the 1960s. The FBI, in collusion with the CIA, and other government intelligence units, spied on American citizens specifically for political reasons. Local law enforcement units maintained spying and intelligence gathering capabilities as one means of trying to combat the social activism of civil rights, student activism, and anti-war demonstrations. These remembrances indicate how law enforcement can be, and is, used for political purposes.

We may not want to believe that our government, as a fact of its existence, uses the police in such a political fashion, inadvertently or otherwise, because it suggests that government may actually be protecting itself from the people. Why would the government want to protect itself from the people it is duly entrusted to serve? The answer may be that it wants to protect its rights of sovereignty from which ultimate and essential political power flows.

To understand why our government feels it must protect its rights of sovereignty, while at the same time maintaining at least the pretense of a consensus model to its politics, we once again need to return to Western societies' recent, past history.

In terms of governmental structures and general social organization, feudal society and modern society had a marked difference. Feudal society had a decentralized form of governance system and modern societies have a centralized form of governance system. What distinguishes the difference? Feudal society had no formal, state governmental structure. That is, it did not have one federal political authority that had ultimate political power over all citizens of the society. The feudalist society had a monarch who held rights over the realm, the territory over which he was recognized as lord and master. All persons in the realm held allegiance to him. However, the monarch did not administratively run his realm. His territory was divided among various subordinate lords and nobles who were given control of certain lands of the realm that were known as estates. These lesser nobles and lords were known as fiefs and their estates were known as fiefdoms. The fiefs, acting with the authority of the monarch, ran their fiefdoms at their own pleasure, and as long as they did not forget their first allegiance to the monarch, the monarch was loath to interfere with the manner in which they ran their fiefdoms or administered the laws of the realm to their peasant workers.

The fiefs performed administrative duties for the monarch and they thereby acted as civil servants for the realm. However, compared to present-day civil servants they had much more independence and power. The feudal system eventually collapsed because the nobles gained too much power and in effect greatly reduced the political strength of the monarch. But with the breakdown of feudalism, modernity began to emerge, and the monarch was able to regain his lost power by developing a centralized governing structure that was based on money wealth rather than the land wealth of feudal economy. This new structure had its own civil servants that were independent of the fiefs. This structure we have come to know in its more developed form today as the state, a federal governmental system.

The new federal state system gave to itself the rights of sovereignty, probably in an effort to ward off any future attempts by the nobles to encroach upon the monarchy's power. Sovereignty meant that the federal, state government had the right to make laws that all citizens of the state were subject to without exception, and sovereignty further gave to the government the right to make people abide by the law with force of arms if necessary. This gave to the federal system, no matter what its ideological posture, the ultimate, essential political power of society. No individuals or groups outside of the federal system had the right to make laws for the entire society. That was something which was left up to the federal government only. This contrasted sharply with the feudal system where the fiefs could, in practical and literal terms, make laws for the governance of their own fiefdom domains and the peasants under their control.

In a much more sophisticated form, we have such a federal system today, which maintains for itself the rights of sovereignty. And since those rights have been written down in a Federal Constitution for the United States and in other subsidiary laws, the rights of sovereignty can be passed from one generation of politicians to the next. Because the federal government has such powers, it can make any laws it chooses and force the citizenry to abide by them under threat of fines, arrest, and imprisonment if they do not. This being the case, it raises some strong questions about the quality of America's free society, as the ethnic minorities have wondered about for many generations, and most recently Japanese-Americans were forced to question under the War Relocation Act.

America has a centralized federal governing structure and this authority tends to guard its rights of sovereignty rather jealously. This seems to result from an inherent tension which exists in America's type of polity. On the one hand, there is a need for a strong centralized governing structure; while on the other hand, our democratic ideology also requires citizen participation in the operation of that structure with the ultimate political power being held by the citizenry. This suggests that there will be ongoing tension in our type of polity between the needs of a strong federal authority and the need for essential political power to remain in the hands of the citizenry.

As well, our history tells us that the forces for a more decentralized type of governance system is still very much present in American society today. States rights versus federal government rights has long been a standing issue in our politics since the founding of this nation in 1776, and the arguments for and against it continue right up to this day. The Civil War and ongoing cultural regionalisms tell us that for some Americans the desire for decentralized governance is still an active force in our society. Indeed the federal government, in an effort not to seem too rigid, has always accommodated these forces, being careful in the process not to give up any of its rights to sovereignty.

Because our federal governmental system professes to operate on democratic principles, it must of necessity lend itself to attempts by the people to possess and use political power as an inherent right of their beliefs in the polity. But government must lend itself to these efforts while not relinquishing its rights to sovereignty. Therefore, the government finds itself being on guard against its own citizenry to protect its rights of sovereignty, while maintaining the appearance that essential political power is really in the hands of the people, the electorate as we like to call ourselves.

This awkward relationship between the government and the people is further exacerbated by the fact that, as mentioned earlier, it is difficult to maintain a consensus model of political decision-making in any case because individuals and groups want decisions to favor them more and others less. There is, for this reason, literally a constant struggle going on in the political process to achieve and maintain a consensus for decision-making. And since government is a distinct party to these negotiations, it finds itself represented as a social element which is also attempting to get the consensus process to favor its positions over those of the citizenry.

Being another contending social element in the consensus process, the government is likely to use whatever forces it has at its command to better its chances for success in negotiations. In this sense, the government can very easily justify using the law enforcement establishment to better its chances for favoritism in the process, and the best justification the government has is that it is the keeper of the sacred traditions. What it does is not for itself, but rather for the good of everyone in the society.

ENFORCING CONFORMITY

As it has been said, it is the responsibility of the police in democratic societies to be suspicious of fringe social elements. They act as a mechanism to pull those individuals who constitute the social periphery, those who operate further from the mainstream norms, towards the social center of society. This statement seems quite complacent and ordinary when applied to criminals. They are obviously operating far outside the mainstream norms and the police have to literally catch them playing out their border deviant politics. But in this context of retrieving individuals from the social periphery, criminals are only a minor consideration. If it were only the recidivist criminals that constituted the social periphery this type of police responsibility would be a simple course of action.

However, the basis for this responsibility lies with ideology and not criminal behavior. Our democracy wants to keep the citizenry thinking alike, being of a like political and ideological mind. It is in this way that the consensus model becomes viable. If certain Americans do not believe in our type of government, its manner of operations, then they are likely to be seen as being on the social periphery. Such individuals could be conforming upright citizens in every sense, except that they may believe that America should have a different form of government, and they abide by their convictions in a non-rebellious way that does not overtly threaten society. Still, on this basis alone, they are likely to be considered ideological outlaws. One only has to recall the McCarthy era and the long-standing close surveillance the police maintained on the people who declared themselves believers in communism, Socialism, and/or Marxism.

This type of police concern can, and does, cut across all social lines, all classes and strata. The rich, the poor, and the prominent can all come under suspicion as ideological outlaws. However, such suspicion is more likely to be showered on those individuals who by the nature of our stratified social system are located socially and culturally away from the social center. Ethnic and religious minorities, and as might be the case with recent immigrants, easily fall into this category. This may imply that the nature of one's lifestyle may cause an individual to be perceived as having non-American beliefs.

What is being stressed here is that the police find themselves concerned with people's beliefs as the part they play in trying to help maintain the political consensus model. The difficulty here is that there is no way that the police, government, or the collective conscience of society could ever know what specifically is going on in any one individual's mind. People are free to express their beliefs. The Constitution of the United States gives us the right to do so, and people are not supposed to be treated differently if their ideas differ from the traditional ideological beliefs. And surely, the intention of the First Amendment makes it clear that the law enforcement establishment should not take the suspicious view of anyone who disagrees with the traditional beliefs. But the needs of the consensus model say something else in terms of what should be the police response to non-traditionalist social believers.

Since most people are not going to get up on a soapbox to express their social and political views, the police, in trying to locate all the individuals who constitute the social periphery, must depend upon behavior as an indication of the beliefs certain individuals may have. This interest fits very well with the police force's basic function of maintaining law and order, which places a stress upon behavior. At the same time, manifest behavior is not the only indication that the police are likely to use in trying to ferret out individuals of the social periphery. They are also likely to be concerned with a citizen's dress, deportment, and general social attitude as this would suggest something different about a person's values, norms, and beliefs.

It would seem, and it is likely to be true, that the police look for any indication of nonconformity among the citizenry as a means of trying to identify social dissenters. And while this does not mean that the police will automatically arrest someone because he happens to dress or act differently than most, still it probably does mean that the police will view such a person differently, most likely in a disapproving manner so as to make the person aware of their suspicion of him.

Now what is being spoken of here has nothing to do with the police reaction to suspected criminal behavior. It is the police reaction to nonconformity that is being addressed, and when the police show their disapproval of nonconformist dress, demeanor, or manifest behavior, through a look, a comment, or the questioning of a citizen, they are letting the person know that he or she is out of step with the norms of society. This is a way of telling the person to move back towards the social center, to conform. An individual police officer may have cause to do this many times during his daily tour of duty, depending upon the community where he works. The fact that the police represent the status quo, their show of disapproval of a citizen is in effect an attempt to pull him back towards the social center.

The police are definitely in the business of enforcing conformity, which may not be so strange for a group whose fundamental job is to catch criminals. Yet it does seem strange since our society professes to be a system that maintains freedom of expression for its citizens. But it is only through the conforming nature of people, in ideas as well as behavior, that makes our kind of polity workable.

Nonconformity in society inevitably brings into question the existing social norms if for no other reason than the fact that alternative beliefs and behavior challenge the status quo, for those who live by the mainstream norms and for those who do not. The average person would seem to prefer not to consciously affirm the norms by which he lives. We seem to be more comfortable with taking our norms for granted in some unthinking, unconscious, gut-reaction sort of way. We are easily brought to anger when there is cause to consider our norms in a better or worse light.

In the 1950s and 1960s, there were the beatnik and hippie movements. The young people involved were posturing new lifestyles that were different from their parents. The public, at the outset, reacted with tremendous hostility towards them, and the police were in the forefront of this abuse. Society gave its sanction to the disapproving attitude of the police towards these groups because the individuals involved were seen as peripheral social elements. The police were given a great deal of latitude in their reproach of these young people because society felt that it was within the police role and function to do so. Who can, or should, best confront nonconformity than the police?

One thing that disturbed the police and society very much about these movements was the manner of dress and cleanliness of the participants. Moreover, the young people tended to have long hair and wear jeans, and they seemed to enjoy mixing in interracial groupings. They were also very egalitarian in their social attitudes. They were not inclined towards the profit motive, the rugged individualist spherics, and sexism. However, they did use certain drugs which society found repugnant, but by and large they were not lawless. Nevertheless, society saw them that way, saw them as ideological outlaws because their attitudes imputed a certain different set of motives for their behavior. The public generally believed that they were socialists or Marxists, which is always a deadly sin in America. If you had to hold political discussions with a Marxist, what's the use? It is impossible to reach any meaningful consensus.

In the early years of both movements, the police were vengeful towards the participants. They raided coffee houses and hippie pads simply because they belonged to such people. The idea was to harrass them and make them feel uncomfortable with their peripheral existence. They were publicly denounced as giving communities a bad name because they were dirty, immoral people, radical in their beliefs. The police verified these common beliefs by spreading propaganda about their nonconforming lifestyles and they were arrested, not for committing crimes, but for trying to live by a different set of values, a different social ideology.

The beatniks and hippies were particularly harrassed by the police because they were primarily middle-class white youths who seem to be forsaking their mainstream roots. Our society is most suspicious and fearful of individuals who once lived by the sacred traditions, but later turned away from them. Their departure from the mainstream might suggest that the values that underlay the consensus model were either not working, or in effect cannot work, or perhaps were never intended to work in the first place. Their forsaking the middle-class lifestyles was a rejection of mainstream norms, and this was, in and of itself, a declaration that they were moving to the social periphery of society.

The exit of middle-class youths from the mainstream was upsetting as a political fact because our democracy is very much concerned with maintaining a political balance to the polity. It is believed that the status quo is best maintained when there is political balance in society, or as the political pundits like to put it, when the politics of the middle road is maintained. Again, this seems to flow from the needs of the consensus decision-making model.

Our society is recognized as having differing ways of viewing the American political process. We have politicians on the left known as liberals, politicians on the right known as conservatives, and politicians who fall between the two called moderates. They all agree on the same fundamental political traditions, but they disagree on how the process should be administered as public policy. It is the balancing of these political forces that allows our system of government to keep a somewhat even, stable course.

It is the conservatives who tend to be, as we said, more for law and order, and in the same way they can be understood as the most traditionally oriented group of politicians. For this reason, they tend to align themselves with the police more often, and the police tend to line up with them more often than with other less conservative politicians. As much as this coalition may occur for ideological reasons, and the fact that it flows from the police function of maintaining law and order, there may be the reason that it is a manner in which the democratic process attempts to maintain a balance in the political forces which is needed to bring about a consensus.

There is a need for the whole of the political process to cultivate an image of moderation. It is from a political position of moderation that consensus is most easily achievable and maintained. This is one of the reasons why the police, although acting out the will of a conservative posture, are required to refrain in large measure from political activities. They are expected to appear neutral. Nevertheless, they are used to maintain a political balance that favors the existing status quo.

Political alignments are also used by the police to help monitor society. In using this alignment, the police are least concerned with the political moderates who tend to be the most conformist of groups to the practical norms of the day. It is those groups on the political left and the political right who are likely to drift to the social ideological periphery. Therefore, the police are likely to become very active in society when the country seems to be drifting towards one or the other of the political extremes. In fact, the case is more true when society seems to be drifting to the political left than towards the political right because of the inherent sympathies of the police to a more conservative posture, but also because a drift to the right tends to confirm traditional values rather than there being a call for the relinquishing of them.

The drift to the left is usually a basic call for changes in the sacred traditions, and covertly a call for changes in the political balance of society. The police are sensitive to behaviors that might indicate this. America's past reminds us of this sensitivity in recalling the police response to the union movement of the last century; the Communist Party during the period of the Great Depression; the Civil Rights and Anti-War movements of the 1960s. In each case cited, the police were being strictly used as a political tool with criminality really not an issue.

Clearly, in those instances mentioned the police were pulling the leftward moving citizenry back to the social center. They may have acted violently at times in doing so, but then democracies are not opposed to using violence to maintain the status quo. The sensitive nature of the police, to public shifts to the political left, was instinctively realized by Richard Nixon, or at least it appears so. He was able to ride into the White House in 1968 on a strong appeal to the return to the values that constituted the social center. He encouraged the police by giving them more authority to stop the social drift to the left. He masked his appeal in law and order terms and an awakening of the silent majority, the heartland of America's true believers.

The police are extremely sensitive to any societal movement towards the political left because it is also a signal of increasing nonconformity as a general style of social behavior. When more and more people restrain their conformity, the role of the police as social managers is made much more difficult. The greater the diversity among the citizenry as a rule, the more difficult the job the police will have in trying to recognize exactly who are the people on the social periphery. This is yet another reason why a police officer's job in the large urban centers is more difficult than those officers who work in small town rural areas. Big cities tend to be crucibles of diversity; whereas in small towns the conformity ratio tends to be much higher.

However, at least in respect to one group, the police have little or no difficulty in determining that they are nonconformist and on the social periphery. The black Americans are stigmatized in this way by virtue of the fact that they are black. Consequently, in terms of maintaining the status quo they are normally viewed as a degenerate social element that naturally devalues the norms of the social center. Blacks are not seen as ideological outlaws on the social periphery. They are pariahs, an outcast people who have no place at the social center. The police are not expected to pull them in towards the social center, but instead are expected to keep them stationary on the social periphery. The police are to be a barrier to their attempts to encroach upon the whites' hold on political power.

The police will normally give greater attention to all communities of the society that are perceived as housing individuals on the social periphery. That is to say that these communities will be heavily patrolled and singled out for closer surveillance. This is certainly true of the black community, but so it is for a bohemian or homosexual community. Not only are these communities watched over by uniformed officers, but they tend to be susceptible to police covert, undercover, plain-clothes work. Again, it is not a question of the amount of crime in such communities, but it is more a question of having a surveillance present in areas that contain nonconformists.

It is the unfortunate occurrence for the black community that it has also been labeled as a community of institutionalized deviancy; or to state it differently, it is believed that the black community, by its nature, produces criminal behavior in its residents. Therefore, there is the tendency of the police to justify the social periphery stigma of blacks on the basis that they are criminally oriented people. This probably is also taken to mean that blacks are innately opposed to the status quo and society's system of law and order. What is not considered is that blacks may oppose the status quo, the system of law and order as professed by our society, because they see these processes as oppressing them. The way the police may come to think of it is that blacks will oppose these processes for their own sake. In fact, this is also the kind of innateness that is attributed to individuals in general who declare themselves to be on the social periphery. They are usually thought to be some type of nihilist or anarchist, for that is the reason why they would be unwilling to conform to society's norms. Nihilists and anarchists are poor bedfellows for a consensus model of political decision-making.

As it has been said, blacks are relegated to a permanent position on the outer borders of society with little hope, as a group, of ever moving into the social center. Yet, according to the American credo, that part which speaks of all men being created equal, at least superficially, they must still be considered part of the democratic process. Of course, the American society has always been ambivalent about its attitudes towards the blacks and it is reflected in the political treatment of them. Nevertheless, the blacks are a large part of the American populace, and in recent years they have held the potential of becoming a possible potent political force.

The American consensus process has always had to be concerned with the possibilities of blacks obtaining full political power. Given the discrimination and prejudice they have suffered over the hundreds of years of their presence in America, with full political power they would very likely seek fundamental changes in the substance of the polity and its operating process. Blacks therefore stand as a potential political force that would threaten to put the American political system out of balance just by the weight of their numbers. For this reason, our society has worked very diligently over the years to keep political power out of the hands of the blacks.

As our society's democratic process has to be concerned with the balance of political forces, it is therefore innately concerned with the possibilities of blacks obtaining full political power. Indeed, an axiom of American politics is that blacks must be prevented from obtaining such power. The police cooperate in this effort by keeping the blacks stationary on the social periphery. One cannot obtain political power if one is not a member of the social center. Even more important, however, is the fact that the police have the power and authority to remove blacks or any other individual from public circulation through invocation of the criminal arrest procedures. Criminals are not allowed to have political power in our society.

Law enforcement officers, as individuals, may not be aware of the political implications of their enforcement policies toward the blacks, but this in no way changes the political impact of it on society. The traditional political balance of the nation is maintained by reducing the chances of blacks to coalesce as a political force. Because the police have the responsibility of being social managers, they are in a unique position to carry out this function for the political process. And there are many ways in which this can be done.

To begin with, just the large number of blacks in America can be seen as an ongoing threat to attempts to maintain political balance among America's contending social forces. For instance in the mid-1960s, there was a great deal of alarmist reporting in the mass media about the possibilities of the blacks coming to dominate most of the large urban centers in the Northeast and Midwest, because the whites were moving out to suburbs and the blacks were moving into the cities from the South. The inner cities became another name for black communities. Also, though there was supposedly no connection between the two, it was further reported that crime was rising to enormous proportions in these same inner city areas where blacks had come to be the dominant, if only, political force.

The society called for law enforcement action to reduce the rising crime in the cities, but this call had the same effect as saying: reduce the number of blacks in the cities, if you will, and thereby reduce their chances for obtaining political power. This was a very normal societal response for two main reasons. First, the blacks, in part, have been maintained as members of the social periphery down through the years because it was generally accepted that they lived in communities of institutionalized deviancy. This label alone makes blacks illegitimate citizens of the society and therefore not fit to participate fully in the hallowed political institutions for a share of the power. If blacks are declared to be innately deviant, or criminally oriented, then this gives license to the police to treat them in a fashion befitting their position. Second, as the number of blacks increased in the inner cities, so did the crime. Reduce the numbers of blacks and you reduce the crime while inadvertently reducing their possibilities for political power.

Therefore, for the sake of reducing crime and covertly helping to maintain political balance, blacks needed to be taken out of circulation. From the point of view of the social center, there was a definite need to arrest and incarcerate more blacks. To be sure, the rates of arrest for blacks did go up in the 1960s and 1970s, with the justification for it being that there were high rates of crime, which just happened to be found more in the black communities than anywhere else in society. Moreover, at the present time the law enforcement establishment is more prone to arrest black males between the ages of 18–25 years of age than any other group in society. It is believed that this group is more likely to commit crimes than any other racial or age group.

It is no wonder then that the prisons and jails of America are filled with black inmates, many of them who say that they are political prisoners. The police are given the social impetus to arrest blacks as a matter of our democratic process, to take them out of circulation in order to keep them from upending the political balance of our polity. This idea may seem to be greatly exaggerated and strange, but one only has to look back over America's recent history and its political relationship to its black citizens to become aware of how blacks, and in particular their leaders, were incarcerated, or even killed, as a means of taking them out of circulation.

It was the United States government that put an end to Marcus Garvey's attempt at political action with his back to Africa movement in the 1920s. Blacks do have a role to play in this country. They are needed to give support to the white middle class. They are not treated equally, but they are wanted for laborer jobs and to do work in the service industries. When economic expansion occurs, they are even used to fill out the employment ranks to keep the industrial wheels turning, and of course they are needed to fight wars.

And what of the questionable causes of the demise of Malcolm X? He was assassinated and the rumors about police-government involvement in his death have yet to subside. And, J. Edgar Hoover of the FBI carried out insidious warfare against Martin Luther King, Jr. for the express reason that he feared King could become a charismatic, political leader for the black masses of America, and in the process lead black Americans on an ideological march to the political left.

It is not the intention here to accuse America's law enforcement establishment of being committed to a policy that causes the assassination of black political leaders, but what is being said is that the police are used distinctly as a political tool against blacks. For instance, if there is any merit to the proposition being offered here, one would be able to notice that not only the police, but the entire criminal justice process, would show this same inclination to further the effort of taking blacks out of public circulation. Or to say it differently, blacks would be treated more harshly than whites or any person of the mainstream. This is a fact of the criminal justice process that has been documented over and over again.

Also, this line of analysis would suggest that the so-called high rates of crime in black communities may be, at least in part, greatly stimulated by police motives. If blacks have been designated to a permanent position on the social periphery, they would normally come under heavy police surveillance. As well, because black communities are declared to be deviant havens, those communities are also thought to require a strong police presence. Just the fact that there are black communities which are being heavily patrolled by the police means administrators will expect more arrests in communities where there are more police on patrol. The more police presence in an area, the more justification for the reporting of crimes and arrests being made.

The greater the police presence in a community, the more directly involved the police will become in the lives of the citizenry. This is obvious if the police have to arrest someone, and what is most interesting about this involvement, is it makes it more difficult for the black community to politically coalesce. The police act as a countervailing force in the community. Their strong presence, from the point of view of the social center, indicates a lack of unity and order among the residents, whether this is actually true or not, and the close surveillance, questioning, frisking, and arresting of residents seem to authenticate a state of instability. It all makes for a weak community basis for political coalescence.

At the more personal level, when a resident is arrested and perhaps incarcerated, it obviously has a negative effect upon the person's family, relatives, and friends. If the person is married, it directly affects his spouse and children. The household becomes a broken home, and food, clothing, and shelter may become more difficult to obtain. Emotional and physical needs go unmet. Children may go without some parental attention. There may be disunity in the family which would hardly be supportive of unity in the community.

The impact of police arrest on a family is another indication of the police being a countervailing force. The police are supposed to be interested in the stability of society through the maintenance of law and order. This means stability at the center and on the periphery. But the removal of a family member, even with cause, creates instability. Specifically, on the periphery this instability helps to anchor the community on the fringes of society, for the societal mainstream expects such communities to be unstable. That is one of the reasons why blacks are kept apart from the social center. The police then are helping to keep the whole of society fragmented between the center and peripheral groups.

In America, maintaining the status quo in the political sense, may not mean having stability of the peaceful kind where there is the absence of social disruption and conflict among societal actors. Maintaining the status quo means keeping matters as they are and in the process protecting the sacred traditions, upholding the political balance, and guarding the social center from the social periphery.

It seems to be clear that there is a natural tension that goes on in democratic societies between the social center and the social periphery, and it is the police who must overlap the breach in serving the interest of the center. It is the perspective of the police to face away from the social center towards the periphery and in the same way the democratic process in trying to maintain a consensus model also takes a similar perspective. This further means that the law and order mandate is directed at the social periphery, and the fate of the status quo is thought to lie in the actions and behaviors of the groups and individuals of that distant area from the social center.

This perspective has caused our society to put an extraordinary reliance upon the police functions of the nation, and this factor has been the inspiration for lawmakers to create a whole body of laws whose purpose is to try to regulate social behavior from a moral point of view. This has given rise to the notion of lawmakers trying to legislate morality. This refers to the body of laws that relate to vice control such as gambling, prostitution, homosexual conduct, and drug control. This has led to what some observers think is an overcriminalization of the law which does not actually refer to criminal behavior, but rather to attempts by lawmakers and their agents to manage behavior and enforce conformity. The fact that this body of law is fraught with administrative problems attests to the covert purpose which they are very much intended to serve. This body of law in particular speaks to the attempts of the social center to use the police as agents for retrieving individuals from the social periphery.

The social periphery of our society is perceived as a threat to our version of a free society, and it is in this sense that government feels compelled to protect itself, if not from all members of society, at least from those on the most outer social and political extremities. Given the role that the police play in this, we can well understand how they have come to be seen as protectors of society. But strangely enough, this is the police being, or government actually being, protective of itself, for our society maintains, theoretically at least, that all citizens have the right to gravitate toward the social periphery if they choose. However, this does not mean that everyone has the right to subvert the present political system, as a matter of free choice, because that kind of freedom would encroach upon the government's prerogatives of sovereignty. Yet, we are still supposed to have the right to move ideologically towards the periphery without committing overt acts of subversion against the central political authority. The right to think freely was thought to be necessary by the framers of the U. S. Constitution to ensure a free and democratic society, but the government has always hedged on free thinking because too liberal an acceptance of this right was, and is, perceived as a threat.

The police stand as an admonishment to anyone drifting towards the social periphery of society. The police will restrain the movement both actually and symbolically as the individual circumstances would require. Police will show their disapproval of all behaviors and attitudes that are not consistent with the norms they are dedicated to maintain, and because they find it more difficult to do their assigned job in the midst of diversity, they will resist a drift towards the borders of society because they will want to try to better their operating role space.

The police, by the requirements of our democratic type of institutions, will be a force in society that restrains the fulfillment of one of our basic political rights—the right to change our mind. And, as the police's perspective is directed towards the social periphery, the view is that the ruination of society comes from that direction, which means that subversion from the social center is played down in favor of subversion at the periphery. For example, the people at the social center often commit crimes and transgressions against society, but their wrongdoing will never be seen as endangering the system as a whole.

Criminals and transgressors from the social center, like white collar criminals, are never seen as a threat to the American system per se, and the status quo ultimately. They are but poor, greedy, misguided persons who overstepped the bounds of propriety, while acts committed by individuals on the social periphery are perceived as being a direct, dire threat, by their actions alone, against the social center. This calls for a stronger response on the part of law enforcement agents against perceived transgressors of the social periphery. By the very fact that some crimes are classified as white collar crimes versus predatory crimes suggests a different police reaction to perpetrators who are either from the social center or the social periphery. It is likely that white collar criminals do more damage to society, to its need for conformity, than the lonely mugger, rapist, or holdup man. The white collar criminal has forsaken his values; the lonely mugger may never have had them.

There is a great deal of propaganda concentrated on publicizing the crimes of the poor and ethnic minorities because their acts, apart from the crimes themselves, also identify the social position from which they emanate. And it reminds those people of the social center that they must be ever watchful of those individuals who live on the social periphery, for their acts can be a threat to society as a whole. To understand this thoroughly, one only has to think of the manner in which mugging as a disruptive social element in society is equated with being the ultimate threat to the system. Having safe streets is equated with freedom in the political sense. Of course, nothing could be further from the truth. A threat to political freedom is more likely to come from within our type of governmental political process than from the citizenry outside of it. Richard Nixon demonstrated that to us.

But because our society has a need to protect itself from its social periphery, it also generates a need to police not only the social periphery, but society as a whole. America is a policed society in every sense of the word.

3

MAINTAINING LAW AND ORDER

I said at the outset of this book that the police have the responsibility
for being social managers. They are expected to maintain social order by
being the on-the-street arbiters of acceptable and non-acceptable social
behavior. The criminal and civil laws are to guide their judgments; which
is to say, the police maintain the law in hopes of keeping order. At least
this is our general understanding.

However, the police are not given this responsibility alone. Indeed,
they are only a part of a much larger process that we have come to know
as the criminal justice system. The police role is very important to the
system because they activate it by arresting and taking people into
custody which results in the citizen's introduction to the process. So
far in this book we have been talking about the role of the police as
the chief activator of the system, but we also need to address some other
elements of the system to see how they relate in their capacities to the
maintenance of law and order, which is the total responsibility of the
entire criminal justice system.

The criminal justice system is divided up among different authorities,
each unit having its own functions, but these individual functions are
interrelated with the systematic tasks of other units. Therefore, the
application of one unit's specific functions is generally systematized
to be compatible with the responsibilities of the others. The criminal
justice system is an interdependent system. The individual units can
function independently, but they are really programmed to operate as
one part of an overlapping series of operations which are triggered by the
police. The influence of the police is therefore felt throughout the criminal
justice process, and this chapter will point out that ongoing influence.

PROSECUTORIAL AUTHORITY

The office of the prosecutor, or the district attorney (the D.A.), has the responsibility of determining what retribution, if any, society should seek against a citizen who has been accused of a transgression. In accordance with the way the process is supposed to work, after a person is arrested for wrongdoing, the next step is to obtain a grand jury indictment, take the case to court where the prosecutor has to prove his charge against the accused before a jury of the defendant's peers. Today, however, an overwhelming majority of criminal cases never reach adjudication. They are settled out of court in a plea-bargaining process in which the accused usually pleads guilty to a lesser charge than the one which was formally lodged against him. In return for the guilty plea, the prosecutor gives certain considerations to the accused such as a lesser sentence than he otherwise might have received, or a sentence in which punishment amounts to being placed on probation rather than being put behind bars.

Of necessity, the police and the prosecutor's office must work closely together. It is the police who make the initial arrest and bring to the attention of the prosecutor an alleged case of wrongdoing, but it is the prosecutor alone who can decide what should be the specific, formal charge which is to be lodged against the accused in court; as well, regardless of the police accusation of wrongdoing, the prosecutor can decide that there will be no charge filed against an accused. If the prosecutor resolves the case through plea-bargaining, the police are not asked to participate in the negotiations.

It goes without saying that the prosecutor has tremendous discretionary power over criminal cases. He can make decisions without necessarily justifying them, and the decisions are practically irrevocable. His is one of the most sensitive positions of social management in our entire society.

Because the functions of the police and the prosecutor are inextricably linked, one might think that the police would be called upon to have more of a say in the resolution of criminal cases, but they do not and with good reason. The police would have a decided interest in seeing that accused individuals are found guilty. Would justice be best served if the police were involved in prosecutorial decision-making? Our society thinks not. Yet, the call of social management would seem to suggest that a compatible relationship is necessary between police and prosecutor. When the police arrest a suspect, they have reason to believe he is guilty of wrongdoing. It is only natural for the police to want to see that the accused person is punished. If the prosecutor fails to punish or allows plea-bargaining to intervene in the case, the police can come to wonder if they and the prosecutor see eye to eye as to the meaning of enforcement of the laws. Difficulties between these two criminal justice units can easily result due to the fact that the police are concerned with the management of public behavior, while the prosecutor must be more concerned with the management of the public's laws.

The prosecutor's office is a political office. The officeholder, at all times, finds himself obligated to a political constituency, regardless of his claims to the free exercise of the powers of his office. In America, the two major political parties, the Democrats and the Republicans, are continually battling each other to get their man voted into the prosecutor's office. The office, in this context, can become a tool of political ideologies, be it conservative or liberal, in the application of the law. But this fight between the two major political parties over the rights of this office is much less important than the use of the office to reinforce mainstream values and the political ideology of the social center against those individuals on the social periphery. Towards this end, the police and the prosecutor's office are compatible.

Still, the police can find themselves hampered by the changing political philosophies that can come to influence the prosecutorial functions. The police would tend to lean towards a more politically conservative philosophy, in the management of the laws, from the prosecutor's office.

It is quite likely that the choice of candidate for the prosecutor's office will be influenced by the individual's attitudes toward the police. Generally speaking, he should be a supporter of the police. Understandably then, a person on the social periphery is not likely to be considered for the office. An individual who becomes a prosecutor will have his roots in the mainstream of the community, and he will want to protect traditional values and maintain the status quo. He is not likely to be a person who would countenance nonconformity and social change. This in itself would give support to police efforts as social managers. We can see this in the following ways.

The prosecutor's office, by its nature, is socially and politically dedicated to supporting the values of the social center. It is the social center which opposes the social periphery. In carrying out his official duties, the prosecutor is likely to be biased in favor of defendants from society's social center. The prosecutor's role can easily take on the posture of protecting the social center from the transgressors of the social periphery. Most of the police arrests come from the people on the social periphery.

At least, in terms of some defendants, the prosecutor can easily come to see his role as being that of punishing transgressors of the law rather than using the office to seek out justice for all. For example, people of the social center who commit transgressions are often viewed as having made a mistake without willful intention. They made an error in judgment or lost their heads and this caused them to stray off the law-abiding track. However, people from the social periphery are likely to be seen as willfully committing transgressions because it is a natural outgrowth of the fact that they come from communities of institutionalized deviancy. It is a normal expression of their lifestyles.

The bias of the prosecutor can be reflected in the way he judges the merits of the evidence, his decision to prosecute or not to prosecute an accused, his decision to seek one charge rather than another, and his willingness to plea-bargain or not. In many other ways, the prosecutor can show favoritism, or a lack thereof, in the handling of cases. When, for example, he seeks indictments, which is a secret process, he can decide to expose or withhold certain evidence, a matter that the criminal justice system leaves entirely up to his discretion.

The fact that there are societal preconceived, negative notions about socially peripheral communities and the fact that the police arrest more people from them than mainstream communities, with the resulting effect of generating beliefs about the inherent deviant personalities of certain social groups, can produce intended miscarriages of justice. More often than not this is a political distinction which works to the disadvantage of a person judged to be on the social periphery. One only has to recall the cases of the Black Panthers, Angela Davis, and Lenny Bruce as examples of the negative treatment accorded accused individuals judged to be on the outer fringes of social acceptance. The Bruce case is particularly interesting because here was a comedian who was harassed and prosecuted by New York City's Manhattan District Attorney's office ostensibly because he was vulgar and used foul language of a sexual nature in public. That was the reason given, in general terms, but he was probably prosecuted because his nightclub act constituted an attack on the traditional beliefs and values held by the social center on sex, race, and politics. He was viewed as a threat to the moral life of the community.

On the other hand, there is a long record of benign punishment accorded to white collar criminals who, by and large, are ensconced at the social center. Take the case of the former City Councilman, Matthew Troy of New York City. Troy was convicted of stealing $36,000 from the estate of two of his elderly clients. Troy was sentenced to spend weekends in jail for six months. His lawyer had the audacity to object to the sentence. The lawyer said his client had been "double-crossed" by the prosecution. To be sure, the prosecutor and judge in the case were not interested in really punishing Matthew Troy. After all, Troy had maintained that he had taken the money because he needed it to support his children. It was not taken for personal gain.

When the prosecution and courts hand out such *unreal* sentences for felony offenses of people from the social center, it has to reinforce the police and society's view of where the real criminals are—on the social periphery.

Let us look at this prosecutorial favoritism from another angle. The prosecutor is likely to see his office as having the responsibility of meting out retribution for his community and that the public he serves depends upon him to punish transgressors as a favor to society. In some ways, he may feel he is forced into this position because his official success is measured by the convictions he can obtain and the number of people he punishes in the name of the community. The public does not want to hear about how effectively he used his office in the administration of justice. They only want to know how many bad guys he put in jail.

The interesting point about this is that the bad guys are not expected to be found at the social center. The light sentences like those given to the Matthew Troy types confirm the belief that good guys can fall prey to errors of judgment.

Since the public is interested in arrest and convictions from the police and prosecutor, there is the propensity among the police and prosecutor not to think about the person who commits the crime, but more about the commission of the crime itself. The prosecutor's concentration is likely to be on the abstract definitions of criminal behavior that is spelled out in the law, and less consideration is given to the human entity involved. Don't think about people, just think about cases.

However, since the prosecutor must seek convictions as a matter of justifying himself as an effective district attorney, he is likely to take personally the decisions he has to make. He may have to think about cases in the abstract, but he will allow his decision-making to be influenced by the demands of the real world. One such reality is the awareness that the people expect the prosecutor to punish those individuals the police arrest. The police believe that they do not arrest innocent people, and they look to the prosecutor to confirm their judgment.

It is the police, more often than not, who do the initial investigation of a case for the prosecutor by virtue of the fact that the police make the arrest and lodge a complaint against the accused. The prosecutor needs to have confidence in the police as the police wish to have their judgments confirmed when they bring an accusation against a citizen. The police and the prosecutor will try to serve each other's needs rather than contest them. This type of interrelating between the police and the prosecutor is not likely to serve the interest of justice for individuals from the social periphery.

The prosecutor also has his own staff of investigators who can initiate investigations or look into cases that are brought to his office by the police. There is a natural inclination, it would seem, for the prosecutor to use his investigative powers to survey those individuals and groups which the community readily recognizes as nonconformists and being outside of the social mainstream. In this capacity, the prosecutor is performing a police function.

Investigating established members of the social periphery is the type of investigative activity by the prosecutor's office that can be very petty and obvious in its intent, and as well frequently exploitative and manipulative by its nature. For instance, a prosecutor may become very active, in the use of his investigatory powers, around the time of re-election. He may pursue a campaign against prostitution, pornography, or groups on the social fringe who operate under different political and social ideologies. In such campaigns, more than likely, he is assured of getting community and police backing which betters his chances, he believes, for re-election. The community will tend to have less sympathy for fringe individuals and groups, and the prosecutor can be very cavalier in his investigation and pursuit of their wrongdoing. If he cavalierly investigated members of the social center, his behavior is likely to be questioned.

The prosecutor uses his investigatory powers to seek out wrongdoing. If that power is turned in on the social center, and wrongdoing is found, this can serve to weaken social cohesiveness at the center of society. For instance, to cavalierly seek out and punish wrongdoing at the social center, in the manner prosecutors may do it on the social periphery, could have the effect of depleting the ranks of those individuals who live more by mainstream values. In political terms, this could have a weakening effect on society's need to maintain a consensus system of politics. This could lessen the social center's hold over the political process, and thereby give the ideologies of the social periphery a better chance to gain ground on the political center.

This political effect can also be seen in terms of light punishments that are given to wrongdoers of the social center. Such transgressors should be given the opportunity to reaffirm their total commitment to the social center. Severe punishment of social center wrongdoers may drive them to the social periphery. This would be a double thrust against the societal mainstream's attempts to maintain political balance between the center and the social fringe.

Keeping in mind the political implications of prosecutorial decisions, as mentioned above, it can be said that the prosecutor not only has the responsibility for punishing convicted individuals from the social fringe, but by his actions he performs an act of ostracism for the social center. This may be stretching the point a bit. Yet, the jails and prisons of this nation are filled with people from the social periphery and not with people from the social center. It is not enough to say that the jails and prisons are filled with individuals from certain social groups rather than others because those groups produce more criminals. To begin with, the police are more likely to arrest people on the social periphery not because of their criminality, but because they reside on the social fringe, and even when people from the social mainstream commit crimes they get off with lighter sentences and are less likely to be incarcerated. Various studies have shown this to be the case time and again.

In this context, the prosecutor is helping to weed out the unwanted individuals of his community. Simply by the manner in which he will treat certain cases versus others, the level of the charge for instance, gives a sign to the judges on bench and the community that certain accused persons are going to get "the book thrown at them" while others are not. It is not for the sake of justice that such distinctions are made, but rather to protect the status quo. If justice means treating individuals before the law fairly, among other things, then the people of the social periphery are not expected to be treated fairly. They are not to be treated with justice to the same extent as people from the social center, and the citizens of the center expect, indeed demand, this unfair treatment. The cries of "get the criminals off the streets" can be interpreted to mean remove people of the social periphery from the community to the extent that they will no longer constitute a perceived threat to the social mainstream.

As the prosecutor's office is being used for social management, and let us say along with that the pursuit of justice and the fulfillment of the law, it has brought about certain problems for the office itself. Initially, the creation of the office was not for social management. Such a design would have been blatantly recognized as undemocratic and more suitable for a police state type of society. Therefore, the office was and is designed to appear as an agency concerned with the prosecution of wrongdoers on an impartial basis. But since the office concerns itself with the weeding out of individuals from the community, inadvertent as it may seem to be, and protecting the mainstream from the people on the social extremities, the office will find itself engaged in the management of people and not just the management of the criminal laws.

As a consequence, the prosecutor's office is involved with the police in enforcing conformity and trying to be a determinant in establishing the moral basis for behavior as expressed by the social center of society. Therefore, the prosecutor will spend a good deal of his time investigating and prosecuting individuals for gambling, nonconformist sexual behavior, radical political activity, drug usage, and so on, which are adjudged to be unacceptable to the mainstream community of society. As a result, the office has become weighted down with too many non-criminal types of cases.

The fact today that the prosecutor's office finds itself overloaded with cases is one of the reasons that is most often given for the widespread use of plea-bargaining. The public believes that this has come about because of the tremendous increase in crime in the last three decades, but it may also be true that the use of plea-bargaining results from the hidden agenda of the prosecutor's office. At the same time, plea-bargaining strengthens the hand of the prosecutor in the management of people. The crowded caseloads of the office have given the prosecutor an obvious reason to use his discretionary powers more, which is conducive to the office's social management role.

What is also quite interesting is the fact that the tremendous increase in the caseloads of the prosecutor's offices coincides with a great deal of political activity by the people of the social periphery in recent years. Perhaps there is more of a correlation to this than has otherwise been realized, in the sense that the prosecutor's office, and law enforcement in general, has had to respond to a greater degree of social managing in the last three decades. The prosecutor's office may presently be overburdened with cases because of society's need for greater social management in recent years than it is due to the fact that there has been an ever increasing rate of crime. The need for more social managing was undoubtedly in response to the demands from the social center for law enforcement to fend off the increasing attempts at encroachment into sacred preserves by the citizenry from the social periphery.

Furthermore, we cannot, or should not, so self-righteously ignore the increasing cries from inmates and social commentators that our nation's jails and prisons may well be filled with political prisoners. This is not to suggest that there are no criminals in jail, but it would be very enlightening for Americans to realize that there may also be many non-criminals in jail. This further suggests that jails and prisons may not necessarily have been made in the first place for the incarceration of criminals, but more for the detaining and removing of anyone who has become a threat to society's social center. Jails and prisons may be in fact precisely what inmates often say they are, nothing more than holding pens.

JUDICIAL AUTHORITY

Formal judicial authority relates to the functions of the court system in the administration of justice. Indeed, it is believed that judges are in fact *the* administrators of justice in the criminal justice process. However, this is not as true as it seems. The police and the office of the prosecutor have much to do with the administration of justice through the use of their discretionary powers in deciding who will or will not be arrested, and who will or will not be charged and tried.

Nevertheless, it is the responsibility of the courts, acting as if they were an impartial body, to oversee the process or trial in which the accused person is given the opportunity to prove himself innocent. The theory for a trial is usually stated the other way around; that is, the purpose of the trial is to prove the defendant guilty, since the legal system likes to maintain the notion that all accused persons are presumed innocent until proven guilty. In truth however, the opposite is more true than not. The fact that an accused person is being brought before "the bar of justice," that he or she has already been formally arrested, indicted, and is being brought to trial suggests that the court litigation is weighted against the defendant, if not on the basis of admissable evidence before the court, then certainly as a psychology among the participants.

In a fashion, this courtroom posture is recognized by the fact that the judge is expected to be a referee between the prosecution and the defense. In playing this role, the judge is expected to give particular attention to the protection of the rights of the defendant in accordance with the law in general, but definitely within the rights granted to the individual under the Constitution. This is thought to be needed because of the enormous power and resources the prosecutor has at his command to the possible dearth of resources that the accused may have to defend himself.

This is to further say that the court is expected to try to give the benefit of the doubt to the accused in respect to the evidence, substantive and procedural law in an effort of striking a balance that will produce fairness in the litigating procedure. It is thought that this would help to equalize the position of the defense somewhat to that of the prosecutor. At the same time, since the trial procedure between prosecution and defense is an adversary one, a battle in which all legal maneuvers can be used to win, the court's position of maintaining fairness is difficult at best, and unlikely at worst, simply because the prosecutor and courts are a part of the same system and the accused and defense lawyer are not.

The court usually finds itself falling into a posture of administrating the procedure of a case rather than ensuring fairness. Fairness is a matter of one's feelings based on one's sense of right and wrong. Each party to the trial process is likely to have his own ideas about fairness. Impartiality is not something that can be spelled out by a law or a procedure. It can only be implied. This means that the prosecution is in a better position of proving his case, given his continuous contact with the court, because he is more likely to be adept at using court procedure than the defense and he will take this into account when preparing his case. Further, it is the prosecution which will be on the offense. The prosecutor is allowed the opportunity, in the first instance, to define the parameters of the case pursuant to the charge that is made. He gets the chance to use his tactics first which gives him the better opportunity to lead the court, while the defense is left largely to react to the prosecution's initiatives. The procedure of the court will normally conform to the procedural and evidentiary tactics that the prosecution wants to take, and this is usually part of a strategy the prosecutor has mapped out before he enters the court.

There is a penchant in the courts to believe the prosecutor and the police more than the accused, if for no other reason than the fact that the police and prosecutor are a part of the criminal justice system as are the courts. They have to work well together, so it is believed, in order that there be proper functioning of the justice system. The accused, one might say, is an interdictor to this process, and the agents of the justice system are likely to perceive the accused in just such a way. As it was said, the elements of the system are expected to work together, but the accused person causes the different agents to assume their systemic responsibilities which can then put the agents at odds with one another as a matter of their functions. For example, prosecutors may disagree with the police and judges with prosecutors over evidence and the handling of a case. The agents of the justice system will attempt to mollify these differences among themselves to reduce the chances for friction. This attempt to be compatible makes for a willingness to accept the word of fellow agents over that of an interdictor.

In recent years there have been a number of decisions by the Supreme Court flowing out of such cases as *Mapp* v. *Ohio, Katz* v. *United States, Terry* v. *Ohio,* and *Miranda* v. *Arizona,* which have reaffirmed the rights of the accused during times of arrest and have acted to restrain police power. These cases and decisions have had their impact on the operations of the prosecutor and the courts and has had the effect of interfering in the relations of the three major elements of the criminal justice system. From the point of view of the agents of the system, these decisions have done more to aggravate the system than to help in preventing or reducing crime. It has caused the police in particular to feel that the prosecutor and the courts were more interested in protecting the rights of the accused rather than punishing the transgressor. There is also a hint in this that the police were feeling that the needed cooperation between the agents of the system was being undercut.

Defendants in criminal cases are to be seen as social deviants whether they are from the social center or the periphery. The justice system takes the view that the accused person is a social outsider. He or she is different from the law-abiding people of the social mainstream, and it could be easily concluded that it is the matter of his or her difference that brought the individual to the court in the first place. That may or may not have been the case, but it still causes the court to look at accused persons as marginal social elements. If nothing else, they are not to be seen as being socially legitimate operants of the justice system, to be sure.

This is all to say that there is a certain bias in the way the court attempts to administer justice which favors the justice system, and by way of the justice system, the social center. It means that no matter how impartial the courts try to be, their search for justice will inevitably favor the prosecution because they are both trying to uphold the values and traditions of the social center. In fact, the closer and stricter the courts hold to the law, relying on only a minimum of interpretation, the likelihood is the more it will favor the position of the prosecutor.

For the reason just given, the court is a protector of the community, like the prosecutor, more than it is an administrative instrument to be used in the search for justice. The courts do see their major responsibility as being that of meting out punishment, and this attitude of punishment is understood in respect to the laws which represent the norms of acceptable behavior. Punishment may be determined as much from the fact that a person deviated from the norms as it might be the result of the individual having been convicted of a specific violation of the law.

A measure of this influence can be understood as occurring because the courts find themselves frequently depending upon non-evidentiary matters in deciding whether to try an accused person, or in deciding what punishment should be handed down for a convicted person. Of course, the court depends upon the police and prosecutor for its initial information about a case, but the court also uses social workers, psychologists, psychiatrists, and probation officers to gather information on its behalf. In using these professional aides, the court, ostensibly, is looking for factors that will have a bearing on the commission of the crime by the defendant and possible reasons for mitigation that should be taken into account when deciding court procedure and, specifically, sentencing.

It is very likely that the original charge which was filed by the police will have an influence on any factors that would seem to suggest that mitigation be shown to an accused or convicted person.

However, while the use of professional aides is most frequently seen as a wish on the court's part to be fair to the accused, such a procedure undoubtedly favors those individuals more who will be adjudged as members of the social mainstream than those who are of the social periphery. The transgressors of the social center will be seen as not living a lifestyle of nonconformity, while persons of the periphery will be seen as being of the opposite. Who will be given the most favorable considerations by the courts, say for probation, where family and community ties are thought to be important in preventing the wrongdoer from getting into trouble again? Why, most likely the wrongdoers of the social center. A judge may interpret reports from ancillary court personnel at his discretion, without any restraint or review from a higher authority.

Consider the enormous amount of freedom the judge has in the sentencing procedure. His discretionary power allows him to favor or disfavor a convicted wrongdoer. Coincidental to this discretion is the fact that the courts have given themselves up to indeterminant sentencing, a procedure which is not well thought of by the police. Persons who are convicted of a crime can be given sentences like one-to-three years, five-to-ten years, or ten-to-twenty years. Indeterminant sentencing is used as an aid to the parole function of the criminal justice system. A convicted person sentenced to prison is eligible for parole when he has served the minimum time of his sentence, provided the inmate is also judged to be rehabilitated. At the same time, it gives the judges a great deal of discretion in sentencing individuals to prison. The punishment is not made to fit the crime, but it is made to fit the person. Indeterminant sentencing has been a tremendous help to this rather social work attitude that has come to manifest itself in the working philosophy of the courts.

Of course, for the more serious crimes the law can mandate a particular sentence that the courts cannot change. For instance, it is not unusual to find mandated sentences for the crimes of rape and murder. But in fact, such cases, regardless of the crime statistics, are only a minor portion of the courts' cases. In most instances, the courts have tremendous freedom in deciding the final sentence a convicted person will receive. Even in matters of plea-bargaining, the judge must approve the deal that is worked out between the accused person and the prosecutor. To be sure, the original charge lodged against a defendant by the prosecutor will in the first stance set the basic parameters for the sentencing, but once the parameters are set, the judge is usually guided by his own feelings, judgments, and prejudices in pronouncing sentence on the accused.

Arresting officers in a criminal case will usually find themselves in court as witnesses against an accused person. In this fashion, the police, through their interpretation of the crime, can have a direct bearing on the attitude of the judge towards the defendant and the specifics of the crime. Because of this, the police can be seen as having some indirect, unofficious input into the sentencing procedure.

Like the prosecutor, the judge too can find himself viewing cases in a very personal light. Judges, by and large, like prosecutors are elected to office. If they want to keep their jobs, frequently it means they have to specifically service particular demands, needs, or even whims of the community. Certainly the interest of the police is also taken into consideration. How judges treat defendants during the trial and the character of their sentences can indeed be a reflection of how they think the community and the police feel about the case, type of offense the accused is charged with, and/or the individual wrongdoer himself.

One of the best examples that can be given of this, as fictional as it may be, appeared in the motion picture *Miracle on 34th Street.* The picture is a tradition on television at the start of the Thanksgiving-Christmas holiday season. The essential element of the motion picture deals with the hired Santa Claus of Macy's Department Store in New York City, who believes himself to be the real, and only, Santa Claus. He is arrested because he is thought to be mentally unbalanced. After all, every adult knows there is no real Santa Claus. The State of New York, represented by the prosecutor's office, wanted to put the man who believed himself to be Santa Claus in a mental institution as being emotionally disturbed, and a competency hearing is held; thus a courtroom drama ensues.

Here was a classic courtroom confrontation between the expectations of social behavior based upon the law, and the practical day-to-day behavior of the citizenry that can emerge from their beliefs. The movie showed how the judge had to be sensitive to what the community wanted regardless of what the law said. Furthermore, the movie demonstrated how some decisions judges make are a reflection of their concerns to remain in office, and that they are not unmindful of the wishes of their constituents. By the way, the Santa Claus was proven to be Santa Claus and the judge was able to satisfy the wishes of the community and keep his job.

Surely, as a person holding political office, a judge will be political in some of his decision-making. There may be no strict consideration of it in many cases, if not most of them, but political decision-making should not be seen only in its narrowest sense. The police in the 1960s were eminently political when trying to combat demonstrations by civil rights marchers, war protestors, and student activists.

When the public becomes interested in a particular court case, like the infamous Rosenberg case of the 1950s or the Angela Davis case of the 1960s, and the judge finds himself in the public's eye, his decisions can become very political. He cannot ignore the community's interest in the matter. By their interest, they have chosen to have a stake in its outcome and such an interest can be influential in the judge's decision-making. Since the public, and this is particularly true in regard to the social mainstream, wants to safeguard itself, it is likely to become interested in cases of wrongdoing that are perceived as being a direct threat to the social center of society. Public interest tends to be most evident when the person who stands accused represents the social periphery in terms of a different political ideology, a different set of values, or a different overall lifestyle that is unacceptable to the social mainstream.

The behavior of judges also tends to reflect their political backgrounds in respect to their party affiliation, Democrat or Republican. But, more than party name, it is the difference in ideology that is to be noted, whether it be of liberal or conservative mold. The police find themselves more compatible with conservative judges because they tend to be more interested in protecting the sacred traditions. These same judges are more likely to show favoritism to defendants from the social mainstream. The situation would not be specifically reversed for judges considered to be liberal, but such judges would probably give a fairer treatment in the court process to an accused person from the social fringe of society. The police are likely to view judges in the latter group as "bleeding heart liberals."

Because of party affiliation, a judge, as inadvertent as it may be, would find himself a proponent of a certain political ideology, and he would be using the court to express that ideology. He can be more or less conservative or liberal, for example, in his interpretation of the procedural laws for the court. The judge alone decides what evidence will be admitted into the court record, and this can have the effect of determining a case's outcome.

Judges are not, nor could they ever be, the free impartial persons that theoretically they are represented as being to the public. They are, by the nature of their function, individuals who have to guard a vested interest for themselves and the community where they serve. Judicial authority is mainstream community authority. And that in itself says that impartiality is not to be a major factor in the adjudicatory process. The community cannot be given its strongest protection from the criminals and noncomformists if the court were truly impartial. To be sure, the court, like the prosecutor, is required to be partial on the side of the acceptable norms of the community. This may not be expressed openly, but it underwrites the entire procedure of the court system's operations.

Further, like the prosecutor the courts are an arm of government and they must work to maintain the status quo and the government's rights of sovereignty over the public. Cases that seem to challenge this governmental authority are not likely to get much of a fair hearing in the courts. That right of sovereignty is a fact of our social traditions and political beliefs; therefore, any person before the bar of justice who seems to represent a challenge to that authority, like a minority individual who feels he is being oppressed by it and consequently must contest that authority, is not likely to be perceived, as a rule, as just an errant social traveler. He may well be perceived as a subversive who is challenging the establishment, and such a person is best removed from the social scene for the good of society. So, we do find our jails filled with people from the social periphery. Yes, some of them undoubtedly were guilty of criminal offenses, but more importantly, most of them are probably guilty of being challengers to the status quo, the traditional political ideology, the government's right of sovereignty. Judicial authority is, and always has been, a biased authority.

JUVENILE JUDICIAL AUTHORITY

Much of the court's time in America is taken up with youthful offenders, the juveniles, teenagers, the non-adult segment of society. While theoretically the criminal justice system is expected to deal with all offenders of the law in an equal manner, if there is to be justice for all, still due to the wishes of society the judicial system recognizes that special considerations need to be given to young people who break the law. The reason seems to be that young people are without the maturity, experience, and adult awareness that would have caused them to be more prudent in their behavior and actions. This is to say that their transgressions can really be the result of mistaken judgment and/or social situations which propel them into deviant behavior that may have been beyond their control, like an unstable home life, specific parental abuse, poverty, or the circumstances of emotional deprivation.

Therefore, the judicial authority has a system of juvenile courts which has the specific responsibility for dealing with youthful offenders in a manner quite different from the way the courts handle the transgressions of adults. This amounts to a tremendous bias in the judicial system towards youthful offenders over adults. Interestingly enough, youthful offenders make up a large percentage of the arrests made by the police.

Traditionally, the cases of youthful offenders are usually adjudicated without the involvement of a jury and a trial. A judge hears the case and frequently the young offender may not even be represented by counsel, but instead a court appointed social worker does an investigation into the nature of the offense, the background of the youth, his previous transgressions, and his general social behavior in the community, such as attendance in school and his circle of friends.

A great deal of weight is given to the social circumstances of the youth beyond the actual consideration of the particular offense committed. It is these other factors that will have much to say about the character of the guilt or innocence of the youth which will in turn heavily influence the judge's sentencing decision. The police record and investigation of the wrongdoing that is alleged against the youth plays a very important role in the disposition of his case.

The prosecutor is largely left out of youthful offender cases, except in the most extraordinary of circumstances. This situation has changed somewhat in recent years in some states where in their larger cities young people were found to be committing the most serious of crimes like that of armed robbery and murder. The result was to lower the legal age for an adult so that youthful offenders charged with the most serious crimes could be tried in the adult courts. In the past the case of a youth sixteen years or younger was automatically placed in the juvenile courts, but in New York City today if a youth is charged with murder his case is not likely to be handled by the juvenile courts. This lowering of the legal age for an adult offender was supported by the police in general, if not specific, terms.

Because the juvenile court judge represents the court, the prosecution, and the defense, the adversary system of justice is relinquished for youthful offenders. In this sense, they are not given the same protection as adults. The judge is the one major decision-maker in the case. All records of the juvenile courts are closed to public scrutiny. As well, the question of judicial review by higher appellate courts do not apply to the juvenile courts, at least in practice. The juvenile court judge is very much his own lord and master in dealing with the cases of juvenile offenders.

The juvenile court system operates around the idea that young people can, and do, make mistakes, but this should not be taken as a sign that young people are incorrigible offenders. In fact, in general, youthful offenders are seen as redeemable. This is obviously more true of youths from the social mainstream. Youthful offenders from the social periphery appear more redeemable as they seem more amenable to the values of the mainstream.

The statements just made about the juvenile court system are obviously generalizations of the way the juvenile court system may try to function overall. It is not necessarily the way the courts will act in every individual case. What the generalizations suggest is that the courts have options and this philosophy forms a basis for the decisions that are generally made in youthful offender cases. In fact, the use of the philosophy is left up to the individual judge.

It needs to be pointed out that the police, particularly those who work in metropolitan areas where there are large populations of youths living in ghettos on the social periphery, take the view that the juvenile courts are much too lenient with youthful offenders, i.e., the police support for the lowering of the legal age for an adult offender. This puts the police at odds with the basic philosophy of the juvenile courts, even in the sense that this philosophy represents theory more than practice.

The juvenile courts have long maintained that a major factor to be considered when evaluating the cases of youthful offenders is whether or not the youngster came from a stable home, and another important factor is whether or not the young person came from a stable community. If the youth were from a middle-class home, and this would suggest that he lived in a middle-class community, he would likely receive the benefits of the assumption that such a home and such a neighborhood were generally stable. In deciding how to dispose of a case of a middle-class juvenile delinquent, juvenile authorities tend to believe that there will be community support to help rehabilitate the youngster, in terms of church leaders, social workers, teachers, neighbors, and various professional types, along with the youth's family.

At the same time, a youth from outside of the social mainstream or a one-parent home, was likely to get the opposite consideration. One-parent homes were traditionally seen as being more unstable and without the necessary parental supervision for youngsters than were two-parent homes. This attitude has been changing of late due to the thrust of the Women's Liberation Movement and rising divorce rates. Moreover, poverty neighborhoods traditionally have been seen as not only unstable, but specifically disorganized. It has been social workers and the police who have been largely responsible for fostering this view of poor neighborhoods on society.

It was believed that a youthful offender from a poor neighborhood would not likely get the community support that would help to keep him out of trouble in the future. Indeed, the court was more likely to assume that to put an errant youngster from the wrong side of the tracks in a rehabilitation center was apt to be for his own good, because in such a center he might receive the support and supervision that was lacking in his community and/or home.

Whatever truth there might have been to this type of thinking, it meant that the juvenile courts had a tremendous bias in favor of one group of youths versus others. This would tell us that as a whole, youthful offenders are not treated as individuals in their own right, but they are treated as objects of a process, a philosophy, which manipulates them for its own very considerable ends.

The philosophy behind the juvenile court evolved from a history of philanthropy and beneficence towards the poor and a desire to protect delinquent youths of the mainstream and disadvantaged youths who were amenable to mainstream values. This philosophy became prominent at a time when the big cities of the North and Northeast of this country were burdened with many children of European immigrants who, because of their poverty it was believed, frequently ran afoul of the law. These young people were initially seen as being ethnically and culturally compatible with America's European heritage and value system, and they were needed for America's growing economy as workers and consumers. They were struggling to assume the mantle of a new culture, and their socialization was hampered by a parental gap of an old-country mentality trying to supervise a new-country way of life. The authorities accepted the notion that these children of immigrant parents were basically good youngsters who found themselves in a socially bad situation. Regardless of the fact that some of them may succumb to wrongdoing, they were expected to take their place in the social mainstream once their assimilation was complete.

When colored ethnic minorities, like blacks, Puerto Ricans, and Chicanos, appeared in large numbers in the big cities and their children ran afoul of the law, they too were introduced to the juvenile court system. But society never intended that they should be assimilated into the mainstream. Society had no place for them there. Consequently, the treatment of the juvenile courts towards them was usually less forgiving. They were seen as members of the social periphery, as intruders in a life-style that was not originally intended for them. Thus, the court's bias tended to work against them and punishment was more their due than rehabilitation.

The philosophy of the juvenile court was also to take into account the fact that young people have a normal penchant to raise hell during adolescence because it is presumed to be one of the ways in which they try to break away from parental control and the domination of their earlier years. The police are less likely to accept this assumption because it bespeaks of their inability to maintain law and order among a certain segment of the population. Nevertheless, adolescent hell raising is seen by the courts and society as a kind of preparation for assuming adulthood. Young people will overstep the bounds of acceptable behavior because they want to declare their independence. Surely, in this sense, the young offender should not be seen as a criminal even if he commits a criminal act, nor should he be thought to be an incorrigible deviant if he goes too far in his perceived sense of performing a rite of passage.

The above mentioned attitude is one that the court might easily take towards white, middle-class, or otherwise mainstream youths. But the attitude would tend to work against youths who did not automatically fall into any of these categories. By the mere fact that the police arrest more juvenile offenders from the social periphery suggests that the courts will take a different attitude towards them. For instance, a youth of the social fringe, i.e., a black youth, who might try to break with his conventions, his social norms, his behavior could be interpreted as that of someone who is trying to break out of the lower social position that society has prescribed for him. He is an outsider because that is the way the social center wants it. His acts of trying to break away from parental dominance and control, his striving for independence, may well be perceived not as a normal act of a youth, but an antisocial act that is directed against society's social stratification system. Therefore, the court could feel compelled to punish such a youngster in order to maintain the status quo and protect the social center.

When New York State lowered the age for adult offenders in order to punish more severely youthful offenders, mostly youngsters from minority group categories, was this not an action that was specifically directed towards youths from the social periphery? It was thought that they were primarily responsible for the rise in street crimes and therefore they were a direct threat to the community. Trying youngsters as adults was intended to remove them from the community for a very long time, until they were less likely to be a threat to the community.

It is in the same context that the criminal justice system maintains an attitude that the most criminally oriented group of society are young black males between the ages of 18 and 25 years old. In more recent years, this age criterion for black youths has been going down overall; while at the same time attempts are being made to change the traditional way the juvenile court system has operated. The general public and the police are supporting efforts to open the records of the juvenile courts and a change for more punishment and less rehabilitation for youthful offenders. These moves are specifically directed at youths from the social periphery because the white public wants them removed from the community. They want these youths removed because they are afraid of them.

All of this can be taken as an indication of how the juvenile courts are being used in the social management of society. In an earlier era, the justice system tended to be lenient with white delinquents, white youthful offenders, because it suited society's overall purposes. Today society does not wish to be lenient with youthful offenders in general, and in particular with youthful offenders from the social periphery. In fact, punishing more severely youthful offenders from the social fringe today is within the same social concern and tradition that called upon society to be lenient with white youths of immigrant families in the past.

There are also indications, with respect to youthful offenders of the social periphery, that the juvenile courts are used as an extension of the welfare system. This idea has to be seen within the frame of reference that the welfare system is in part a mechanism by which the social center maintains a permanent underclass in society that is not wanted in the mainstream. When one thinks of the welfare system in this light, then it is not a give-away program as the conservative politicians like to describe it, but it is a means by which society attempts to keep those individuals who have been relegated to the social outhouse apart from the mainstream of society. Welfare clients need public assistance in order to economically survive, and they are given the bare minimum of assistance to live on, for without it they might turn on the social center and become committed revolutionaries. The welfare system basically does not operate to serve the interests of its clients, but rather the interests of the social mainstream in that public assistance helps to keep the groups of the social fringe in their peripheral places.

In this context, welfare programs are a part of society's institutional techniques at social management. When the police and the court make distinctions between juvenile offenders based on what is best for the community, rather than what is best for the youth, then this is social managing. When the court decides that one youthful offender should be reformed and rehabilitated in an institution and another is to be reformed and rehabilitated in his neighborhood, this is social managing in the same way that public assistance is used.

There is also a free and easy relationship between the welfare system and the juvenile court system, if for no other reason than the fact that the welfare system is run by social workers and social workers have a large role to play in the decision-making of the juvenile courts. In some ways,

the fact that children who happen to be on welfare are found to be frequently entangled in the juvenile court system may have something to
say about the close relationship that exists between social workers of
the welfare system and the social workers of the juvenile courts. But
more specifically, the reason relates to the fact that the social work
ideology of helping people pervades the juvenile court system. It helps
to hide the court's operations of social management, and it is also an
impetus for judges to act beyond the law in a personalized, judgmental
fashion. They justify the personalizing of their actions with reports
from ancillary personnel like social workers and psychologists who advise
the judge to take a certain action for the good of the youth.

Judges who fall under the spell of social workers and psychologists tend
to get bad grades from the police. The police tend not to be very respect-
ful of these two professions when they are allowed to intervene in
criminal justice matters, even when the accused person happens to be a
youth.

Of course, the ideology of social workers will have its influence in
general on cases that come before the juvenile courts, but it will be disadvantaged youthful offenders who will be subjected to it most. Middle-
class, white, mainstream youthful offenders are to be redeemed more
readily with the help of their stable family and community lifestyles.
Disadvantaged youthful offenders are to be helped in spite of their unstable family and community lifestyles. If the disadvantaged youthful
offender is on welfare, this attitude towards him will be even more certain. The ideology is being used to extend control over one group of
offenders while seeking to relinquish control over the other. This suggests
that disadvantaged youthful offenders are seen as being out of control
because of the social circumstances surrounding their lives and the
more affluent youthful offenders are given the benefit of this idea in
the opposite direction. Consequently, institutional rehabilitation would
seem more a proper alternative in one case, and not in the other.

Juvenile justice, inadvertently one might say, gives recognition to the
importance of young people to society in whatever future the society
will have. It is the young people of today who will be the dominant
voices of society tomorrow. Showing deference to youths from the social
center over those from the social periphery has the effect of helping to
ensure which youths will have the best opportunity for moving into
important, decision-making roles of society. Our society is very biased
against people who have arrest and/or prison records—which makes the
police important in this context also. To identify a youth as a lawbreaker, a nonconformist, can have the lifelong effect of excluding him
from some of the most important, and some not so important, positions

our society has to offer. Many important business, government, and political positions are thought to be too sensitive to take chances of employing someone who has run afoul of the law and already shown the potential of abrogating the norms and values of the social center.

Whether the juvenile courts acknowledge it or not, their activities will have social and political ramifications for many youthful offenders when they reach adulthood. And in trying to understand the workings of the juvenile justice system, we should not be overly influenced by the mass media's descriptions of the court. The mass media will report on the most unusual cases handled by the court, like a youth being held for murder. As a consequence, the public is left with the idea that such cases are the rule rather than the exception in the normal day-to-day operations of the court. Nevertheless, these cases are small in numbers. What the court does more often than not is make decisions for errant youths who have taken cookies from the proverbial cookie jar, or were rowdy in the streets, or were out late, standing around on corners, or possibly were caught smoking pot, or committing some prank act of juvenile delinquency. And it is in these matters that a juvenile court can, and undoubtedly often does, strike a political blow for the social mainstream.

PROBATION, CORRECTIONS, AND PAROLE AUTHORITIES

After an accused person has been convicted of breaking the law, probation may be given to the individual in lieu of putting him in jail. Such a decision by the judge is usually based on certain presumptions. To begin with, the judge is likely to believe that incarceration is not the best alternative for the person because he is probably not perceived as a hardened criminal. Second, it is probably thought that the person will try to avoid getting into trouble again, and that he is of such a character that will submit to supervision by a probation officer. Third, the person will acknowledge his wrongdoing, and in doing so hold to the terms of his probation because he realizes that by not doing so the judge could still put him in jail.

Most of these presumptions, if not all of them, will have to be satisfied in the judge's mind before probation is likely to be given. In terms of these presumptions, a judge has a great deal of latitude; or to state it differently, he can be quite capricious and arbitrary in allowing or not allowing probation. As well, his judgmental freedom is further used in setting the conditions of the probation—the length of it, the frequency of reporting in to a probation officer, or not requiring any reporting to an officer.

Such decisions on probation are made independent of the law that was violated and the punishment called for in the breaking of the law. In fact, the decisions are made more as a matter of the judge's discretion than anything else. Furthermore, it is unlikely that such decisions will be amenable to judicial review by an apellate court, although that does remain a possibility, provided that either the prosecution or the defense make such an application to a higher court. In any event, the review is not likely if the case does not deal with a capital offense.

Frequently, the police have voiced their dissatisfaction with the freedom the judge has in allocating probation to individuals they may feel should have been incarcerated because of the seriousness of the crime for which they were found guilty; or because the police may feel that certain convicted persons are likely to commit future crimes. Still, a judge does not have to allow himself to be influenced by these police concerns, although he may well be, when allowing probation for a convicted defendant.

A probation officer will most often make an investigation of the background of a convicted person before the judge renders a decision in a case; which is to say that the probation officer can influence the judge's decision by his reporting on the lifestyle, job status, family background, etc., of the convicted person, irrespective of the evidence presented in the case. The probation officer will be looking over the circumstances of the person's life with respect to the possibility that he or she will be amenable to probationary supervision. Like the judge, the officer can be somewhat free in his interpretation and evaluation of the social circumstances he uncovers. Initially, the probation officer may base his investigation on the information given to him by the police from the original accusation report.

Before recommending probation, an officer will probably want to be satisfied that the convicted person can be supervised with the least amount of difficulty. Like most of the operants of the justice system, probation officers also tend to be overburdened with cases. Probations are alternatives to incarceration, and when the prisons are crowded, the courts are likely to view probation more favorably. It has been well documented that our nation's prisons have been overcrowded for a long time. The result is increased caseloads for probation officers and attempts by them to ease the pressures of their supervisory responsibilities over probationers. One of the techniques a probation officer may use to ease these pressures, which is used during the investigation period, is that of looking for social elements in the background of a candidate that are much like his own, or at least elements that the officer can relate to and perhaps identify with. Social similarities between the officer and the probationer would seem to suggest that supervision would be easier for all parties concerned.

Like the prosecutor and the judge, the probation officer will tend to see himself as a public servant, working for the well-being and protection of the mainstream community. As a result, he will more readily recommend probation for persons who, in spite of wrongdoing, still maintain a faith in the core values of society's social center. Such persons can be considered good candidates for probation because they are not likely to have ties to the social periphery. Indeed, they are probably even more likely to have a distaste for the values and lifestyles of the fringe segments of society.

Probation officers will not as readily recommend probation for individuals from the social periphery because it is believed that the people from such environments make a habit of being deviant and contesting the established structures of authority by the nature of their social position. To return a person to that type of social environment would not be a good probationary risk. Indeed, it may be thought that whenever a wrongdoer from a socially labelled negative community is given probation instead of incarceration, there is the possibility that this acts as an inducement to the wrongdoers and others of the same community to commit further anti-social acts because of the expectations of minimal punishment. The police certainly believe this to be true.

Many persons convicted of crimes do receive probation. However, many persons convicted of crimes do go to jail. As it was said, our jails and prisons are overcrowded with inmates. At the same time, if sentencing and probationary exercises do favor certain groups and individuals over others, one would expect to find our prisons primarily filled with individuals who are from the social extremities of society. And thus this is the case. Our prisons are filled with people from ethnic minority backgrounds, the poorest whites who grew up on the fringe of the mainstream, and the complete criminal incorrigibles of all racial types who, for whatever their reasons, are not fit for community lifestyles at the social center or the social periphery of society. These are the social rogues found among any social group, but they are always a very small minority as a function of the human genetic pool.

Correctional officers or prison guards are in effect and in fact jailers in the most onerous sense of the term. Like the police they tend to see their job as that of protecting society from the bad guys, the convicted criminals. They also tend to believe that the inmates they guard have cancelled their right to live in the public domain because of their conviction for criminal wrongdoing. Correctional officers, even more than the police on the streets, find themselves, on a day-to-day basis, face to face with some known, hardened criminals. For prison guards, inmates are not just people who have made mistakes, but rather inmates are apt to be seen as social mistakes in themselves, as rogues, as wild hairs who have mustang spirits that have to be broken. Because of this perception, there will be a clash between the guard and the inmate personalities in the prison environment. Success for the prison guard revolves around his abilities, he believes, to denude inmates of their toughness. A very interesting point is that during their tours of duty, prison guards are as much in prison as the inmates.

Prison should not be taken as an alternative community type of life-style for people who have made mistakes in society, but it should be understood for what it really is, a jail, a lockup, a house of cages which are expressly in existence to restrain and control inmates. Penal authorities view inmates as feral individuals who, like animals in a zoo, have to be put in cages to prevent them from giving into their wild urges; for these are people who cannot control themselves, who are self-centered and think of themselves as being so important that laws and norms were made for suckers and dopes. The police would be in full agreement with this view.

As a consequence, prison guards will take the position that inmates of prisons are being punished because they asked for it. They were given the same chance as anyone else to conform to the laws of society, but they either chose not to or they did not have the wherewithall to restrain themselves from committing criminal acts. Either way, it was their own individual behaviors that caused them to cross over the threshold into the incarcerated world of the prisoner's life.

Correctional officers, the prison guards, do not give much credence to the idea that some inmates may have been wrongly imprisoned, that some are in fact innocent of the crimes they have been found guilty of. All inmates are thought to be guilty of a criminal offense. That is why they are in the lockup. For the prison officer, that is an ultimate reality that must be faced. Inmates are people who are different than the average person out there in society. They march to a different drummer, one who has a beat that rotates counter to the norms of society. Spiritually they are different and the spirit that brought them to prison must be broken if they are to return to society to live a normal life. Penal authorities take the position that inmates have to learn to submit to authority. They must give up their self-centered toughness and accept the fact that they must abide by the laws of society.

Like other operants of the criminal justice system, prison guards accept the fact that they work for society, the mainstream community. They believe that they are protecting society from disruptive social elements by guarding the criminals in prison. Therefore, it is not surprising to them that most of the people they detain in their prisons are ethnic minorities and "white trash," as it is sometimes put. Certainly, it is the people of the social periphery who would be, by their nature, disruptive social elements in respect to the norms of the social mainstream.

In regard to this belief, the general attitudes that correctional officers will have about inmates are those that society has in general about people who have been relegated to a life on the social periphery. It is the nonconformity and incorrigibility of inmates that disturbs prison guards the most, and not the criminal acts that put them in prison. Once the particular criminal act has been committed, it is over and done with. Nonconformity and incorrigibility can be ongoing. Clearly, correctional officers and police officers have similar attitudes about wrongdoers and people on the social periphery. Prison guards may in fact actually think of themselves as being law enforcement officers and not just correctional officers, but the two roles are not interchangeable, even though they have their similar means of expression.

The penal system holds an unusual position in society. Prisons are seen as existing apart from the general social structure. To be sure, prisons are seen as being outside of society, as though they are holding pens, so to speak. For this reason, inmates are recognized as having been rejected by society. Going to prison is a form of ostracism. Consequently, prisoners have to work their way back into society through time served and indications of rehabilitation by being submissive to the authority of the penal institution where they have been incarcerated.

Very few prison inmates actually serve out the full sentences given to them at the time of trial, that is the maximum of their sentences. Most sentences are given with minimum and a maximum number of years, one to three years, five to ten years, and so on, as was pointed out previously. In any event, even when a convicted person is given a flat sentence, as for murder, for example, he is still likely to receive consideration for early release based on good behavior or definite indications of rehabilitation which would seem to show penitence for past transgressions.

An inmate can be considered for a parole, which means early release from incarceration to the supervision of a parole officer, once the minimum part of his sentence has expired. In many areas of the country, parole and probation officers are under the same authority. This tends to be the case because the supervisory technique for a probationer and parolee is about the same. The paroled inmate will usually remain under parole supervision until he has completed the maximum time of his sentence.

The police tend to be very skeptical of the parole system. It places too many recidivist felons back on the streets to commit more crimes, and the police believe that their job is made more difficult as a consequence. The parole system tends, from the police's point of view, to be guided by misplaced humanism and sympathy.

Parole is granted to an inmate by a parole board or a commission, which is a group of individuals, usually appointed by the governor of the state, who sit as an independent body apart from the penal system itself. It is their responsibility to review the prison record of inmates, once they are eligible for parole and decide, at their own discretion, whether or not the prisoner has been rehabilitated to the extent that he deserves readmittance to society outside of prison walls. There are few specific guidelines to help parole boards make a decision to release an inmate early, other than the board members' own judgments and perceptions, and their word is usually final. What the board seems to look for in making its decisions is an indication that once the inmate is released, he will be law-abiding, and will conform to the social center's norms. This may require the inmate to adopt new values, new behavioral patterns, and the more willing an inmate seems to be in striving to make these changes, the better chance he will have in being granted a parole.

To be sure, inmates come to know what the parole board expects from them, and that is what they try to demonstrate during the parole interview. Since the parole board members cannot possibly know what is going on in the candidate's mind, they depend upon factors such as appearance, demeanor, demographic background and former social circumstances of the inmate, and his probable community associations if returned to society to help them make a decision. Given these criteria, if the inmate was a member of the social mainstream before incarceration, he is likely to be given the benefit of the board's doubts at the outset of a parole interview. This is a decided plus for the inmate.

Contrarily, if the inmate's past community relations were of the social periphery, he is likely to start his interview with a minus. In other words, for the convict with the plus the parole board will likely try to look for good points in the person's record that would be helpful to him in obtaining a parole. For the inmate with the minus, the board would likely need more convincing of his suitability for parole. Further, the same psychology exists for the parole board as it does for probation officers who seek probation for a person presumed to be amenable to supervision. Parole board members will surely take into account the chances of success or failure with each parole granted, since it forms a record of the ability of the board to perform its assigned task with good or bad judgment.

Parole board members know that they have a sensitive role in the criminal justice system, in that they decide on whether or not to readmit a convicted felon to society. They are made aware of the records the police keep on the high recidivism rates. Therefore, what can be of prime importance in their minds when evaluating an inmate is not his actual rehabilitative status, but whether the parole will be good for society. For instance, parole boards have been accused of using their function as a means to control prison populations. This has a bearing on the actions of parole boards in that they are a part of the social management team of society. If boards feel they must release a certain number of prison inmates to relieve overcrowded facilities, their decisions are bound to be based on criteria that go far beyond the rehabilitative status of inmates.

Since they have the best interests of the mainstream community in mind when making their decisions, the board will probably be favorable to inmates who specifically bear the imprint of the mainstream of society rather than those who bear other social imprints. They will not want to release inmates from prison, as a function of overcrowded facilities let's say, if they believe that such persons will drift back into habits of a socio-peripheral lifestyle, which would not necessarily, in their minds, be good for the mainstream community of society. They would probably want to put back into the community people who they think will be conformists rather than nonconformists.

Ethnic minorities are not likely to fair well compared to other inmates when prison population control is a consideration in the determination of parole. Ethnic minorities will be seen as returning to the periphery of society and its community of institutionalized deviancy. Why should such inmates be released on parole as a factor of relieving prison population pressures, if in turn it means increasing the pressure on society from the social periphery.

It is highly unlikely that parole board members do give conscious consideration to these points, but they are nevertheless suggested by the habitual release policies of these bodies. The first to be incarcerated is the last to be repatriated.

The judgment as to whether an inmate is ready to return to society is greatly determined by the position the inmate held before he entered prison. This type of concern does not flow from the law or a consideration for justice, but it is a result of social management. Moreover, it is not a concern that is guided by what is best for the inmate, but by what is perceived as best for society. What is best for society overrides all other considerations in the operation of the probation, corrections, and parole authorities. They may be separate authorities but they are all bound by the same ideological concerns which interrelate their functioning. It is their duty to serve the interests of the social center of society.

PERPETRATOR AND VICTIM

The criminal justice system is made up of a series of authorities and these authorities are generally bound together by overlapping functions. What also helps to bind the various elements together is a rather bifocal view of society. The justice system takes the view that society contains good guys and bad guys, perpetrators and victims. There are the police crime reports that seem to justify this view. The perception greatly influences the manner in which the criminal justice process operates, and it probably has too much influence on the system. For instance, this perception can come to generally affect all the operants of the system to the degree that they begin to see it as a normal state of nature. Therefore, the criminal laws, police, courts and judges, and prisons are also accepted as a natural need of human societies. There must be strong-armed social managers to keep the bad guys from taking advantage of the good guys. The difficulty with this attitude is that it soon makes cynics of us all. We lose our faith and trust in our fellow human beings. We come to fear them as they come to fear us, and this is particularly true for those people who work in the criminal justice system.

Having reached a high level of cynicism, the operant of the justice system then is likely to impute a certain self-righteousness to himself and the process for which he works. The job to be done requires the belief that the justice system, even with its problems, is still essentially a good system. Moreover, since the justice system draws its strength from the values perpetuated at the social center, these values, even with their contradictions, remain as indications of the essential good of society as a whole.

Furthermore, the good which is natural in the world comes to be accepted as what the community and the criminal justice system stand for, and the bad, naturally, are represented by those social elements that the community does not stand for, or rejects. As our culture also teaches that good, and this the Bible tells us, is forever being beseiged by evil, the attitude likely to complete this belief system is one that society must always be on guard, and that is why there are police and other elements of the criminal justice process.

If society represents the good, then it is society that is under seige from those evil forces that are natural to human environments. The great problem with this kind of thinking is that once one decides that certain social elements are good and that they are being opposed, one must also determine, define, and describe the other elements which are bad. Under this system of thinking, society will define evil as a matter of need and not as a matter of the evil acts which are done.

It is easy to take this posture if one views society as being in a struggle between people and social forces at an acceptable center, and people and opposing forces at a social periphery. Perhaps this says something to us about why certain groups are delegated to the social periphery as a result of the stratification system of our society. And these individuals, by and large, who look different from people at the social center can easily be identified as possible sources of social opposition. Generally, these are the colored ethnic minorities and also individuals who are nonconformist and ideologically out of bounds with the mainstream attitudes and norms.

The criminal justice system takes the position that those people who break the law are perpetrators and the victim is society. Therefore, perpetrators are those social actors who willfully act against the best interests of society. At the same time, people who reside at the social periphery are thought to be in opposition to the social center of society, under the adage: "If you're not with us, then you must be against us." This tells us that the criminal justice system, by its very presence, furthers the notion that there is a struggle going on inside the social system at all times between the perpetrators and a victimized society.

Of course, the criminal justice system uses the idea of the ongoing struggle in society to justify its existence. It does this by quoting crime figures. However, it is not crime, the breaking of laws that is specifically being addressed; rather, it is the idea that society is under seige. It is a call for society to get more police, pull in its flanks and protect itself, to be less liberal and more conservative. To prove to the public that society is under seige, while adding to its justification for existing, the criminal justice system will arrest more and more "criminals" until literally the jails are filled to overflowing with the perpetrators.

When our society feels most threatened by internal social forces, these are the times when the prisons will tend to fill up rapidly with perpetrators, not criminals. And there undoubtedly will be cries of a rising crime rate to match the rising police-criminal justice system activity. We only have to recall the 1960s to be made aware of this type of social connection. Time and again, allegations were made, and mostly ignored, that the police were instigators in the riots and street violence which frequently occurred during protest demonstrations during that period. The public was not to be taken in by these allegations. If the police overstepped their bounds, they did so under extreme provocation in most cases.

Yet, police instigation can be seen as a logical extension of society's need to prove the existence of perpetrators within, and to remind the public of the ongoing struggle in society. The idea of the ever-present perpetrator, and the actors therefrom, is used to give support to the actions of the criminal justice operants. Therefore, during times of social stress, when society feels under siege, the activities of the criminal justice system are likely to increase, with greater severity in sentencing, longer periods of incarceration, and outright police vigilantism. We had this situation during the depression years, when our society was seen as being under attack by bank robbers, mobsters, and communists. However, a clearer picture of the time indicates that the lawless 1930s was greatly exaggerated; yet, it was a time when law enforcement and the criminal justice system was expanding, particularly at the federal level.

The criminal justice system nurtures the public's awareness of the perpetrator for its own self-serving interests. The public, when aroused and agitated over the presence of the perpetrator, will turn its attention to the social periphery, for this is the segment of society that is generally thought to be the area that produces the criminal element. Once again, we can see how this occurred in the 1960s when the criminal justice system put out the word that society was falling prey to criminal elements. There were many reports that serious crimes were rising at a very rapid rate. The public associated these reports with the social activism of the period, and out of fear, turned against any and all people on the social periphery, like the blacks, Puerto Ricans, Chicanos, Indians, hippies, student activists, and other nonconformist groups. For the criminal justice system, it did not matter that the notion of criminal behavior was being stretched to cover any form of non-traditional protest. The system was able to increase and expand its activities with the sanction of the societal mainstream.

The point to be made here is that reports of criminal wrongdoing are not a good or fair indicator of criminal justice activity, but rather the notion that society is under siege. For example, throughout much of the 1970s the crime rates were as high or higher than the mid1960s when so much fuss was made about them. Indeed, as crime has risen in the decade of the 1970s, police activity has fallen off considerably. If anything, it seems that the criminal justice system, or society overall, has become more tolerant of crime. The 1970s, however, did not see the parades of demonstrators in the streets that made the public feel that society was under siege as was the case in the 1960s.

It seems rather clear that the criminal justice system is more interested in maintaining a characterization of society as being a victim to the ever-present perpetrator than the system is interested in individual acts or crimes or specific categories of crimes. Crime refers to the breakage of laws by individuals, but the idea of the perpetrator refers to society being under attack by evil forces, forces as the Bible would tell us that are dedicated to destroying the good in the world. Since these forces are natural to the human environment, there can never be a total solution to the problem.

Following this line of thinking, the social periphery, as it may be seen as the force behind the perpetrator, is therefore destined to be always with us, which suggests further that matters which nurture it will always be with us. This attitude complements the general sociological view in our society that poverty produces crime and the poor will always be with us. Racism, prejudice, and discrimination are normal to human groups because of the innateness of ethnocentrism; consequently, certain minority groups who are of the social periphery will always be with us. And since these groups constituted a designated place on the social extremity it also says that they will always be people who in themselves constitute a force that can besiege society. Therefore society must be on guard against them, and the criminal justice system must give very special and particular attention to these groups, if society is going to have a chance to survive in the long run, despite the incursions that will be made by them, like those which occurred in the 1960s.

The criminal justice system has a great deal of freedom in nurturing the awareness of the perpetrator, the police taking the lead in this effort, but it has even more freedom in directing the attention of society towards those areas and groups from whence the assault upon society is coming. This is accomplished by reporting which social groups are arrested more than others, which seemingly spells out for society the particular groups that commit the most crimes.

Crime statistics are used to tune in the social mainstream to the source and movements of the ever-present perpetrator. It is not surprising to note that the statistics constantly tell us that the siege is coming from the permanent members of the social periphery, the poor and the minorities. We are reminded of the FBI profile of the most likely person to commit a criminal act: a black youth, age 18-25. Crime by definition is an act of violence of one person against another. It is the felonies of robbery, assault, burglary, mugging, predatory crimes, and the like that are emphasized by the crime statistics. It is the image of blacks and other minorities attacking whites of the social mainstream, the good law-abiding citizens, that the statistics tend to imply.

This confirms the social center's fear and apprehension about the people on the social periphery, while it also clarifies the fact as to why the police and the criminal justice system are so active in respect to certain social groups and not others. It also furthers a discretionary role of decision-making and activity in the criminal justice process, for example, the wide use of plea-bargaining as a means of getting convictions without a trial by jury. The message that the prosecutor and the courts transmit to the public for their wide use of plea-bargaining, in the face of the fact that it circumvents the constitutional rights of the accused, is that prosecutors and court calenders are too crowded with cases. Plea-bargaining is justifiable because it takes some of the pressure off the prosecutor and the courts by not having to go through a trial for every accused person, and it saves the public money. But the obvious problem with this explanation is that it allows the prosecutor and the courts to determine, and/or accept, the guilt of a person. Yet the guilt is not proven as an exercise in the administration of justice and it is actually determined by administrative fiat.

If the prosecutor and the courts are motivated to judge certain groups differently than others, then the process of plea-bargaining will definitely reflect this. For instance, it is the prosecutor who determines the price for plea-bargaining; that is, he sets the level of the charge that the accused will be asked to plead guilty to in lieu of facing a trial. The prosecutor and the courts have almost an absolute free hand in this. It would not be difficult to understand that if the court is biased towards the social center and against the periphery that the price for plea-bargaining will be lower for one group and higher for the other in overall terms. When crime statistics are reported to the public, such as convictions of certain types of crimes for certain groups, the role of plea-bargaining in the numbers is not explained, and therefore the public's view of which group commits more crimes and the most serious crimes, can be very much in error.

It is said that plea-bargaining is supermarket justice and that it favors the criminal. There is truth to this, but only if one assumes that the criminal justice system is in business to deal strictly with people who break the criminal laws and who are in fact criminals of the recidivist type. But if the basic purpose of the criminal justice system is primarily social management, then this so-called favoritism can also be seen as a means of furthering the labeling process of who are the perpetrators of society, and from whence in society they come. Plea-bargaining inflates the crime statistics and enhances the view that there is a struggle going on in society between the center and peripheral groups.

The need of the criminal justice system to identify groups of individuals on the social periphery as placing the society under siege is an ongoing fact of the process, and is done so as a normal expectation of the system. Take this example: A New York City police officer once pointed out to me that in the early 1950s, people of Hispanic backgrounds, like Puerto Ricans and Cubans, were considered by the police to be white. However, by the latter years of that decade, the crime statistics for this group were reported to be rising sharply. Forgetting for the moment that these figures may have been inflated, the New York City Police Department was greatly concerned because the rising crime rates among Hispanics were driving up the statistics for whites in general. This could give a different color to the face of the ever-present perpetrator, at least in New York City. Needless to say, the New York City Police Department changed its reporting procedure and Hispanics were no longer considered to be white.

Supermarket justice can, and does, have its negative effect upon the criminal justice system. If the system is loaded down with a certain bias, as I have been discussing, it is not necessarily a conscious factor in the minds of the people who operationalize the system, and it does not have to be. It is a function of socialization and habit which has produced expectations of how certain groups should be treated as a matter of the norms of society. Police officers, prosecutors, and judges would object vehemently to the idea that they are biased. The police believe that they only arrest bad guys for the good of society. Therefore, when they arrest someone who they believe has broken the law and that person is subsequently released from jail, or given a reduced sentence, as a result of plea-bargaining that is not commensurate with the crime for which he was arrested, they can feel that the courts, or the system is defeating its own purpose, and indeed making their efforts worthless.

This results in part from the fact that the operants of the criminal justice system, like people in general in society, function from a taken-for-granted attitude about acceptable norms of behavior in society, for themselves and for others. But at the same time, we can and often do challenge our own taken-for-granted attitudes when and if they do not seem to satisfy our personal needs at a given point in time. But this does not mean that we give those attitudes up, or that we necessarily want to give them up. The taken-for-granted attitudes are realized as a function of the group, and our participation in it. We can disagree with the group, but that does not necessarily mean we want to withdraw entirely from it because that would amount to self-ostracization. Such is the case with our taken-for-granted attitudes.

In the same fashion, supermarket justice can cause the public, looking from the outside in, to be confused about what the criminal justice system is trying to do. The public likes to believe that criminals are caught, and if convicted, put away in prison for long stretches of time. But when plea-bargaining returns a felon to the streets in a very short period of time, the public can come to think of the system, the courts particularly, as favoring the perpetrator. But in part, the public may assume this attitude towards the criminal justice system as a fact of its own sense of human failing; that the system is being asked to do social managing to maintain social order, when it is the job that we the individual citizens must grapple with rather than trying, as a society, to delegate that function to a designated elite group. While we tacitly uphold the purposes of and the need for the police and the criminal justice system, we can also become wary of the institution. The police particularly are always crying wolf at the door. It would make us all feel a bit more socially comfortable if we were not being continuously told that the ever-present perpetrator was lurking on the social periphery. At the same time, it is one of the specific functions we have delegated to the police, and we may have done so because we suspect that the wolf at the door may be confronting a wolf in the house.

THE POLITICS OF CRIMINAL JUSTICE

The criminal justice system is an arm of government, and its expressed purpose is that of furthering the social policies, of a formal and informal nature, of the social center. The social center is greatly represented by government, and government is seen as representing society as a whole. Therefore, government and politics are greatly involved with the operations of the criminal justice system. Of course, the connection is even more direct in that government makes laws and it is the responsibility of the criminal justice system to maintain them. Furthermore, since the police are used to penetrate the lives of citizens in a watchful manner, as an outcome of the consensus decision-making model of society, politics is natural to the operations of the criminal justice system. Along with this, there is what can be called the politics of criminal justice, which is the use of the justice system by politicians specifically for the vested interests of the social center.

The politics of criminal justice is ongoing, but the citizenry tend not to notice it when there is social tranquility. When there are social upheavals buffeting society, the politics of criminal justice will stand out boldly. Again, the most recent example of this was in the 1960s when a confluence of social forces and social activism seemed to converge on the social center with the intent of undercutting the traditional values and political operations of this society: the Civil Rights movement, student activist movement, the hippie movement, the Women's Liberation Movement, the gay rights movement, the anti-war movement, and a general political left attack on what was euphemistically called "the establishment."

One of the ways society responded to this perceived threat, which in many respects was no threat at all, but rather the democratic process trying to make itself work, was to set new priorities for the criminal justice system. The system was given a mandate to develop a more uniform national front to defend against insurgency. The federal government in 1968 passed the Omnibus Crime Control and Safe Streets Act, which was expressly designed to drive demonstrators from the streets. The police were given questionable powers to arrest demonstrators, not because they might commit crimes, but because they were political agitators.

The federal government set up a new bureaucracy to coordinate a united front against criminals and the source of general social unrest, the Law Enforcement Assistance Administration (LEAA). The new agency financed improvements in facilities and increased manpower resources to drive back the insurgents. Law enforcement personnel were encouraged with scholarships and grants to increase their education, almost as a means to fight off the intellectual arguments against the system which had developed from some of the so-called radicals of the left. Sociology and psychology courses were made mandatory for many young police officers and trainees because the character of the struggle was as much ideological as it was physical.

The widespread involvement of the news media in the social activism of the day required that law enforcement personnel be able to use the newspapers and airwaves to defend themselves against the actions taken in defense of society. Police personnel had to be schooled in the political notions of socialism, communism, anarchy, and nihilism, for this was the best way to classify and describe the push coming from the social extremities, descriptions that were specifically used because they readily identified the philosophies of these activist groups as being different from the social philosophy of the social center.

And, as the insurgents were defined by various non-American ideologies, to sharpen the struggle, there needed to be a description of the forces that wanted to maintain society in its traditional pattern of functioning. As a consequence, a new term came into being, "the silent majority," which referred to the conformist people of the social center who were not demonstrating against traditional authority, and indeed who were the people ready to defend the system against the insurgents. The police were their soldiers and the police knew exactly who they were fighting for and who they were fighting against. With a clear political line established, it made police efforts to quell the insurgency easier.

The politics of criminal justice was made starkly clear by a social factor that was mentioned earlier. There suddenly appeared all across the nation the "law and order" candidates who sought office on the basis of defending traditional America against the wave of anti-Americanism that was coming from the social extremes. The best known of these types of candidates was Richard M. Nixon who became president and Frank L. Rizzo who became mayor of Philadelphia. They represented a type of politician who was saying that he would stand behind the police to push the social periphery back to where it belongs—out of sight and out of mind. As Richard Nixon's vice president, Spiro Agnew, put it: "If you've seen one ghetto, you've seen them all."

Given the gravity of the situation, as society saw it in the 1960s, the politics of criminal justice was blatantly exposed for a time. More often, however, this process is covert. The criminal justice system can be used by politicians to serve vested interests by shaping the laws and criminal justice policies.

It should not be forgotten that laws serve those who promulgate them. People on the social periphery rarely if ever obtain a politically significant office, an office that can have some impact on society overall, or even in an individual local mainstream community. Consequently, the act of promulgation will favor those who are of the social center because they will hold the important political offices. The in and out groups of political office are practically ordained by our society's reliance on laws as the means of maintaining social order.

The fact that most criminal justice personnel are either elected to office, appointed to office, or selected for their positions through ostensibly competitive examinations, also speaks of the political nature of the system. This also holds true for the police although they are normally not seen in this light. Police are thought to obtain their position by competitive civil service examination. But it is the politicians who direct the civil service and determine the nature and character of the exams. That the examinations have been suspected of being politically weighted is pointed out by the fact that on a number of occasions minorities seeking positions on police forces around the country have sued civil service commissions, seeking relief in the courts. They have charged that the police exams were frequently biased in favor of white applicants over minority applicants. The civil service commissions have generally maintained that the police exams are fair. But, obviously, politicians want police officers serving the community who have their view of society rather than individuals who do not. The police exams are used to further this end, and it has its own discriminatory logic as unconscious as it may be.

Prosecutors, police commissioners, judges, wardens, and parole officers are all political people, and so their functions in the criminal justice system can also be seen as being political, or at least as being politically tainted. It would be difficult to imagine that since they do owe their positions to the political arena, this would not be reflected in their work. In New York City, the police commissioner was expected to run his department in accordance with the political ideology of the mayor. John Lindsay, who was mayor of New York City during most of the volatile years of the 1960s, had some difficulty with his police commissioners because he had a liberal ideology which he tried to instill in a police department that normally functions from a more conservative ideology. If police commissioners, as appointed officials, do not follow the ideological line of their political masters, they are usually relieved of their responsibilities.

All the major decisions of the criminal justice system are made by politicians. It is the mayor of the city who holds sovereign rank over the justice system's budget, and the hiring or firing of its personnel. Through budgetary control, the politicians can set priorities and promulgate policy for the system. Budgetary control gives the politicians the ability to reward or punish the system as the executive branch in charge sees fit. Therefore, if the politicians want the police to conduct a certain kind of surveillance, close scrutiny of the social periphery, it is not difficult to manage it as a policy through a system of budgetary priorities, or as an outright mandate based on the giving or withholding of funds.

In the 1960s, the federal government, through LEAA, used its ability to dispense millions of dollars to local law enforcement agencies as a means of promulgating a national policy for the direction criminal justice would take throughout the nation. This was a political design devised by the Nixon administration, and if local law enforcement groups had qualms about the policy, since some of it was legally doubtful on constitutional grounds, they forgot their inhibitions because they wanted the money.

Clearly, criminal justice is a manipulative, sociocultural, political tool that functions at the behest of this society's central authority. To misconstrue this, to play it down, will leave us with a completely errant understanding of what criminal justice is all about. If the criminal justice system did not serve society's central authority, it would have no essential reason for existing. It is the central political authority, the government, which puts life into the system with laws, policies, mandates and money. Without the operating substance, the system would collapse, or never have been born in the first place.

Government, as we have seen time and again, is not a neutral social entity. It has its own interest, obligated and preferred. It has vested interest, interest in maintaining the sacred traditions that give it operating life. The laws that are made by government are to ensure its interest, to serve its needs. To think otherwise is just to ignore the realities of human social life. It is ridiculous for us to believe that laws were meant to be, or ever could be, neutral. Laws come into existence to serve a purpose and not to be neutral.

Surely the criminal law was not meant to be neutral. It was intended to oppose certain social behaviors that society declares unacceptable. Laws are measuring sticks by which individuals are judged, and because laws exist they bring into being certain attitudes. The need for general surveillance over the citizenry is one of these attitudes. This is surveillance not only by law enforcement but more importantly, it is surveillance we extend over ourselves. We have learned to oppose our own inclinations of behavior out of fear that we might be breaking the law.

The police remain as the most obvious potent reason for us to stay inside of the law; for they are ongoing governmental, political representatives in our neighborhoods. We may see them at any time, day or night, from the windows of our homes, and we can hear the sirens of their squad cars as they go racing through the streets to corral some errant social member who forgot, misstepped, or took a chance on the belief that he would not be found out, not be caught by the surveillance network that is thrown over the entire society.

Watch everyone is the police officer's motto, but the central political authority is more concerned about some groups than others. Within the social center, surveillance is at a minimum, and in the social periphery it is at a maximum, and there is a grid that flows from the center to the extremities with ever-increasing surveillance as the grid moves outward from the social center. And the use of raw police power will increase with greater abandonment from the center to the extremities, and such gradations will have governmental, political approval in relation to the secure or insecure feelings that manifest themselves within the social mainstream at any given time of this nation's history.

If government makes laws for the specific reason of opposing certain behaviors, at the same time those laws legitimize other behaviors. We should well understand at this point which is which. The law by its nature approves of the behavior of some, while disapproving of the behavior of others. For those individuals and groups whose behaviors are acceptable, they are being stimulated by the law to continue their acceptable behavior and stay inside the norms, but for those individuals whose behaviors the law might oppose, they are being stimulated to stay outside the norms. Indeed, the expectation of the law is likely to force them outside of it.

Such a proposition does not happen by design. It is not the work of crafty politicians of extraordinary conservatism, or discriminatory or prejudicial persons in government that brings this about in the body of this nation's law. No, the laws are just a representation of our society's values and its sacred traditions, and it is these social attitudes that we have come to express in the laws of the land. To put it most simply, it all comes about as a matter of tradition and socialization. At the same time, an individual's personal motives or prejudices cannot be totally excluded from the equation as influential modalities.

That there is bias in the operations of our customs, bespeaks of what is the nature of customs, and that bias is clearly represented by the overall discretionary nature of the way the laws are carried out and promulgated by the criminal justice system. This discretionary impetus can be challenged on its own merits, as it reflects the social customs of our nation, customs that run afoul of our own expressed democratic ethos of equality for all before the law.

But this is a strange bind for any society to find itself in, because customs are preferential. They include and exclude, by the nature of their existence, not only between different societies, but as it has been shown, within the same society itself. Customs form the basis for a social center and the springboard for a social periphery. They set the premise of political institutions, for the basic character of governmental operations in the formal and particularly the informal sense. They bind people and political institutions together as a matter of the taken-for-granted attitudes of citizens.

It is custom, in the final analysis, that binds the various authorities of the criminal justice system together, just as it is custom which binds the criminal justice system to the central political authority and the public to the government. Laws in and of themselves cannot do this, except as they represent the acceptable procedure of custom. By the same token, it is difficult to ferret out much of the reason and purpose for the criminal justice system responding as it does to political authority because it is buried in the years of unthinking, unevaluated, habitual custom. Custom makes certain attitudes and behaviors right because they are a matter of custom. Citizens should abide by the norms of the social center because it is the social center. In the minds of the people of the social mainstream of society that is reason enough to conform.

After all is said and done, this kind of simplicity of judgment is behind the manner in which the criminal justice system functions and society overall. It allows for extremely biased decisions to be made towards favored and unfavored groups by the operants of the system. Yet, it can still leave them with the feeling that the decisions made were right, correct, and unassailable. This simplicity is buried in the body of the law because it also affects the governmental, legislative process. It is a function not of individuals but of society and the culture that supports it. The perpetrator walks the land because we believe it. We believe that we must have armed shock troops to protect us from the perpetrator. *What we believe, becomes what is.*

4

THE POLICE AND SOCIETY

The police exist as a societal mechanism. Yet, it is an interesting fact of modern American life that the police are perceived not so much as being a part of society as they are perceived as being separated from it. The police and the criminal justice system are seen as being above society on a higher, loftier plain. This perception is due in large measure to the responsibilities that have been allocated to them, the maintenance of law and order and all that that entails. But this fact also speaks to our dependency on them, and it is quite common for humans to think better of those individuals and social elements on whom we find ourselves dependent.

Society has then placed the police in a privileged position as initial arbiters of right and wrong behavior. We have given them the authority to threaten, coerce, arrest, and even kill us if we do not abide by the laws of which they have become guardians. This means we are at the mercy of the good faith and judgment of the individual police officer and the collective power for which he stands. We want the police to be society's conscience on the street, walking and talking like Jiminy Cricket. This is an awesome responsibility, one that is in the practical sense unassumable. The police can never be for us what we are unwilling to assume for ourselves. In fact, there is some question as to whether we actually accept the police in this role or we as society just pretend to. Individual citizens are just as apt to criticize the police as to praise them, not because the police succeed or fail as law enforcers, but because they are asked to be an everyday conscience for society, in the right or wrong behavioral sense.

The view of the police as separate from society is a natural consequence of the development of a centralized government system that came into being with the demise of feudalism. The governance structure of modern society is distinctly separated from the rest of the social system, and the police as an arm of government is thence a part of that structure. But unlike the rest of government, the police must work in society with, and among, citizens on a day-to-day basis. The work of the police is actualized directly and only in terms of the citizens. This means that police work is heavily dependent upon the attitudes of the public concerning the work it does, i.e., the right of the police to have authority over them where they must make judgments about the behavior of citizens. Without our acceptance of this authority, our system of policing would surely break down hurriedly. The ghetto riots of the 1960s made that point perfectly clear, and suffice to say the public's attitude toward police work is as important to the policing of America as are the attitudes of the police officers themselves.

COOPERATION

Under our present system of policing, in order for the police to carry out their assigned responsibilities they must have the cooperation of the citizenry. Before the police can intervene in lawbreaking and wrongdoing, they must first be made aware of its occurrence. More often than not, it is the public that makes the police aware of such occurrences because the police are so small in numbers, compared to the total population. But all too frequently, the public is unwilling to report the occurrence of wrongdoing unless it is of the most serious nature, and not always even in such a case because to become involved with the police means to acknowledge, if not capitulate to, their higher authority. In a true sense, this is not cooperation because one person must give way to another, the citizen to the police. It is a belittling exercise.

At the same time that the police are dependent upon the citizenry, they think of themselves as having authority over the citizenry, which is indeed true. But to be dependent upon the citizenry in order to express that authority means that the cooperation the police need does by its nature delimit that authority. If they do not have the proper situation in which to express that authority, which usually comes about because of a report from the citizenry, it then remains moot.

To be sure there are times when the citizenry want the police to take charge of a situation. When citizens find themselves confronted with violent persons, who may even be armed, they are willing to let the police officer risk his life to control the situation. Or if there is an extremely nasty family situation that has gotten out of control, again citizens appreciate the police taking over. But more often than not, one's encounter with the police is more likely to be with a traffic summons, or some type of public behavior that is not criminal in nature, but still prohibited: gambling, drinking in the park, fornication, or the like. Here morality can become the issue and the police in stepping in to prohibit the behavior may be thought of as encroaching upon a citizen's individual personal rights. Our type of policing gives the police the right to infringe upon what we consider to be our personal rights—the right to govern our own behavior, just as long as it is not specifically and purposefully infringing or injurious to other persons.

But since the police are called upon to maintain social order, their concern has to be with various types of behaviors that may disturb that order, even if the individuals involved did not expressly intend it for that reason, i.e., public drunkenness, loud unruly behavior during the early hours of the morning when most people are asleep. The fact that the police do intercede into societal behavior that is a matter of morality causes the public to be wary of the police, and they frequently do not want to cooperate with them out of a feeling that they will compromise their own sense of self, decision-making and purpose to that of the higher authority of the police.

By training, the police are taught to deal with situations from a position of domination and control. They are trained to believe, and by their experience of fulfilling their social commitment they come to believe, that they must take charge of a situation when they become involved. It is a matter of maintaining police authority, but it is also believed that since they are called into situations where there may be wrongdoing, taking charge is the only way to come to the proper decisions on what needs to be done, the invocation or not of the arrest procedure.

Periodically, the police will push campaigns to get the public to be more supportive of their efforts to fight wrongdoing in the community, and they tend to be somewhat mystified as to why the public is so hesitant about giving them their support. The police see themselves as trying to protect the public from criminals. So then, why wouldn't the public want to help on their own behalf? In part, certainly, this passivity is a result of a general malaise throughout society that is seen in terms of politics, voting, and just keeping the streets clean, but it may also have something to do with the fact that citizens do not like the control that they may fall under when the police are asked to intercede into a social malfunctioning situation.

This is not to speak in terms of the wrongdoing of a citizen behaving in a criminal manner who obviously does not want the police involved in what he is doing. This relates to the victim. It is the victim who can have reservations about cooperating with the police and for reasons that go beyond the mere reporting of a wrongdoing. For instance, when a person reports a wrongdoing and calls for police assistance, the police expect the person to stand by the allegation as a witness, and indeed if the accused is brought to trial, the victim can be subpoenaed to testify in court, if necessary against his or her will, with the threat of imprisonment for the victim if he or she fails to appear as a witness.

This in itself can and does turn away many people from involving themselves with the police. It is the initial meeting with the police, that first time of initiating cooperation that can be very irksome to the public. The police by nature are accusatory, not conciliatory; blamesetters, rather than blame-relievers. They enter into a situation where at the outset everyone is a suspect until the facts are sorted out, if they can ever be sorted out. From a citizen's point of view, this is an odd basis for cooperation because it means that the person is putting himself at risk as a possible suspect.

Police across the country will tend to rate communities in accordance with their perception of the cooperation they can or cannot receive and this helps to form the basis for the types of behavior that the police will demonstrate to the people of different communities. The police perception of community cooperation starts at the social center and proceeds outward. And there is a basis in fact for this. Police attitudes on cooperation favor the communities of the social center because they are more likely to cooperate with the police than the people from fringe communities. This cooperation is encouraged by the fact that the communities at the center are given credit for certain things like innate honesty when reporting crimes and the people on the outskirts are not allowed the same assumptions. But this can be a problem for the police.

The police are less wary, less suspicious of the people at the social center, which means such individuals can get away with more wrongdoing initially because the police will be less suspicious of them. The people at the periphery are likely to get away with less because initially the police are more suspicious of them. This is interesting because the level of social wrongdoing is thought to be much higher in the communities at the social edge than at the center. It suggests that there may be higher rates of wrongdoing at the social center than is normally thought of, but it may remain undetected, underreported, or not reported at all. And the reverse may be true for the opposite reason at the social periphery.

At the same time, there may also be a great deal of crime not reported from the social periphery because individuals of those communities have a basic reservation about calling in the police. They are aware of the suspicions the police tend to have about them because they are outside of the social mainstream. When one adds the color factor of certain minority groups, they will definitely fade away from involvement with the police because of this. Too, cooperation with the police is likely to be perceived as supporting the police in the efforts to control the peripheral communities for the benefit of the social center. It is not surprising then that the strongest accusation of lack of citizen cooperation with the police is directed toward ethnic communities, and the accusation seems ambiguous because these same communities are reported to have the highest rates of crime.

While the type of policing of our society does require cooperation by the citizenry, the police specifically seek it, by their own admission, because they say it makes their job easier in catching criminals, of course. But to make their job easier in this context is to make police presence and control more widespread through society. In terms of preventing crime, this would seem to be a good thing. But if crime is really not the main game plan for the police, increasing their influence in society does not necessarily serve the best interest of all the members of society, excluding the purely criminal element. And indeed, such influence would be proportional to center-periphery relationships. The fringe elements of society are likely to come under greater pressure from the center if there is greater cooperation with the police.

An indication of this became somewhat evident in the 1960s and 1970s when police departments around the country spent a great deal of time and money to set up community relations squads and offices to better the cooperation between colored minority communities and the police. Police community relations activities were a direct response to the activism of minority communities in the 1960s. Better relations between the police and these communities were broadcasted as the way to prevent future riots and to give better protection to the residents.

There was no comparable effort made in white middle-class communities, and from all indications the effort worked to cool off the communities because over a period of time greater police presence and surveillance, with local residents helping, staved off the political activism that had been occurring in those communities. Community relations programs helped to increase police control over black ghettos in particular. And to further this effort of cooperation, more black cops were hired, frequently with community agreement. Black officers made the increased control through better cooperation more palatable for the residents.

Seeking greater community cooperation from the social fringe, while at the same time not seeking it to the same degree from the social center, is a means of pulling in the social periphery towards the social center. If such communities can be made to feel that the cause of the police is their cause, then the job of the police is made easier. But in actual fact, the police used community relations programs to spread their influence, collect information, and to keep tabs on certain individuals and groups, like the Black Panthers, the Black Muslims, and Chicago's Black Stone Rangers.

These police community relations efforts were accomplished at a cost of reducing the police's criminal law enforcement effort. Indeed, community relations programs tended to obviate a police concern for crime prevention in minority fringe communities. Crime was less important to the police penetration of fringe communities in the name of cooperation. To be sure, politicians were firmly behind this police effort, often forcing such programs on police departments against the will of the departments' commanders. But once the activism of the black community was effectively blunted, these community relations programs tended to become less important or disappeared as a police focus altogether.

The community relations programs also had another effect upon black communities in particular. During this period of bettering relations, the police were encouraged to be more cooperative with the black community. This was translated on the streets by the police to mean being more tolerant of blacks' behavior, even if it was inconsistent with acceptable societal norms, short of serious criminal behavior, as a means of staving off police and black community confrontations. In large urban black communities, the tolerance took the form of allowing blacks to affect the lifestyles of their choice, as long as it was kept in their own communities. If they chose to be deviant, then so be it. The tolerance, in fact, was giving recognition to a social policy of long standing for communities of the social periphery. Deviancy was tolerated to a much higher degree at the periphery than the center because the people on the fringes were seen as being deviants.

For instance, gambling, public drunkenness, drug usage were openly accepted in the black ghetto because it was rationalized that the community accepted it. In actual fact, the police tolerated these wrongdoings because it made their jobs easier in the ghetto. Drunks and drug addicts could be handled easier than a person who had his full wits about him.

And numbers playing was tolerated because it gave the poor people something to hope for in financial rewards that they were not likely to get from the menial labor jobs that most of them had. This type of police tolerance was a means of encouraging such behavior, and not too infrequently the police were getting paid off for looking the other way which further encouraged this behavior.

Seeking cooperation from the citizenry is the police's attempt to bridge the gap that naturally exists between them and the people, but the seeking is really used to further police control and domination of social situations. That control and domination is directed outward from the social center and the pressure to obtain cooperation increases as one drifts further from the mainstream. The measure of this cooperation can be understood in terms of the needs of the police to survey and control certain communities as compared to others. Interestingly enough, the communities who should have less support for the police are expected to have the most, and they are socially condemned for not having it.

Cooperation means to give oneself willingly to participation, but in a real sense, the difference in authority of the police to the public makes such cooperation impossible. However, it is an entirely moot point in any event because the police actually use the call for cooperation as a tool in the policing of the social periphery. To that end, the call for citizen support for the police has been successful, at least when it has been specifically directed at the communities of the social fringe in recent years.

SUSPICION

Nothing points out the separation that exists between the police and the public more than the gulf of suspicion that exists between the two. As guardians of the public peace, the police are required to be always on the watch, on the lookout for behavior that would be disturbing to the maintenance of order. Therefore, they maintain a suspicious eye over all that they survey. At the same time, the public is aware of the police presence and purposes. Individuals do not want to fall under police surveillance and certainly do not want to be arrested. The police are seen patrolling, looking for wrongdoers. Since a citizen cannot read a police officer's mind, he can never know what a police officer is thinking and whether or not he is being considered a suspect. Therefore, members of the public are likely to be suspicious of the police because they believe that the police are naturally suspicious of them. The level of suspicion varies from one social status to the next, increasing as one moves further away from the mainstream.

It is society, the citizenry through government officials, who have given the police their authority. It is we, the public, who have given the police the responsibility to be social managers, but this is not to say that society is at all times happy with the authority and power the police have. In fact, having a society that attempts to work by democratic principles, that seeks freedom of expression for its citizens, this in itself would probably produce a suspicious posture towards police authority. There are enough examples from the 1960s that indicate that unchecked police authority can easily become police power that is abused, i.e., the Chicago police riots of 1968.

When the police are used specifically in a political role, this can quickly arouse public suspicion. At times, this suspicion can be just as heated from the social center as from the social periphery. While the police do concentrate their attention on individuals and communities outwardly from the center, they also react to any questioning of their authority from any quarter of the society. The social center can be very sensitive to police authority, even when it is not used abusively towards them, because the center is considered the guardian crucible of America's credo, its democratic principles and societal freedoms. The citizens of the mainstream are acutely aware of the dangers of unchecked police authority and power. They are not unmindful of the fact that if the police are allowed to operate uncontrolled and in a cavalier fashion against the social periphery, such power could also be turned on the social center.

When the police, for example, rioted in Chicago in 1968 and forcibly demonstrated for higher salaries in New York City in 1976, their animosity and wrath were very much directed at the social center. In Chicago, for instance, newsmen and politicians were beaten, along with the yippies, in the police efforts to stop any demonstrations in the streets. In New York City, the police demonstrations were specifically a confrontation with the administration of Mayor Abraham Beame.

The social center, because of the credo which gives it political and philosophical meaning, and which the police are dedicated to protect, finds itself being suspicious of the police because of the bonds which bind the two together. The suspicion results from the fear of unbridled police power producing a fascistic or totalitarian state. Because the center has this concern, it has attempted to put restraints, by law, upon police power. This has taken the form of trying to protect the rights of citizens when confronted with police authority and power.

By and large, it is believed that these laws to protect the rights of citizens benefit most individuals on the social periphery, but clearly these protections are a hedge by the social center at protecting itself from unbridled police power. For example, the police are bound by the law not to stop persons, any person, on the street for questioning purely out of a matter of suspicion. This can amount to an interrogation of citizens, although it may be done openly on the streets. Traditionally, police have maintained that this was necessary in terms of deciding what course of action to follow with a suspect. But the courts have asked, what was the person suspected of doing in the first place? Often nothing specific, except that the person looked suspicious to a particular police officer. If the person is suspected of committing a specific crime, that is a clarifying reason to stop him and question him.

Just the right of the police to stop and question a person, because an officer may feel like doing so, can be understood as an abuse of police authority, and if left unchecked, who knows where it might lead? And it is not only the matter of police stopping individuals and interrogating them, but the police have also been known to stop and frisk a person on the streets because he looks suspicious to them. This is search, if not seizure, without any real probable cause. The procedure became a particularly tense issue during the 1960s because it did seem as though the police were taking liberties with this exercise in the minority communities. Their zealousness, it was said, was a result of the social activism that had been going on in those communities during the period.

The right of the police to opportunistically frisk citizens was contested in the courts, which is the way grievances are handled at the social center. The Supreme Court rendered a decision on the matter in 1968 in the case of *Terry* v. *Ohio*. The Court held that the purpose of the frisk should be that of looking for weapons on a suspect who might use such weapons to endanger the police officer. Frisking should not be used to search for evidence on a person before that person has been formally arrested. Frisking should not be a witchhunting expedition. Once the person has been arrested such a search for evidence can proceed.

Frisking is more likely to occur in socially peripheral communities because they tend to be communities perceived as being filled with probable wrongdoers, and because frisking is also likely to be the result of intense police surveillance. The more intense the surveillance, the more likely the frisking. As the social center may encourage such surveillance on the one hand, it can very well fear it on the other hand. Since the social center's initiations inspire greater police surveillance of fringe communities, this means that the social center in this context is feeding its own fears.

The police, of course, do initiate investigations on their own suspicious volition. In matters of crime, frequently the areas delved into come under the heading of vice; for example, prostitution, gambling, and narcotics. What is interesting about these areas of investigation is that they are thought not to produce victims as innocent parties to the activity, but it is believed that the perpetrators themselves are the victims. Such areas of wrongdoing are not habitually brought to the attention of the police by members of the community, but more frequently the police take it upon themselves to initiate investigatory action. These areas could also be described as including behaviors that specifically reflect moral values, or a lack thereof. These types of investigations can therefore be seen as police attempts to cleanse the social periphery of immoral behavior, and to pull those people involved back towards the social center.

The police may use a number of different procedures when initiating an investigation like covert surveillance, searching private property, electronic eavesdropping, and undercover operations. Of course, for a democratic society that prides itself on the rights of privacy and free speech, these are very scarey tactics for the police to be using, tactics that can easily get out of hand. Under the Nixon administration, law enforcement used such procedures illegally against political opponents and people of the ideological social fringe. Because such procedures can easily fall into abuse and misuse, the social center has sought to have specific restraints placed on this type of activity of the police which historically are backed by provisions of the U. S. Constitution.

To search a person's home or private premises, prior to arrest, is illegal without a search warrant issued by a judge or the permission of the person who owns the property. The Fourth Amendment of the Constitution guarantees the individual freedom from unreasonable searches. Further, in 1961 (*Mapp* v. *Ohio*), the Supreme Court said that evidence improperly seized could not be admitted into a trial. Now this sounds all well and good, but frequently the people who are most likely to fall under unruly police behavior are not aware of their rights. The educational system and society has benignly failed to inform them. Plus, whenever activities, or suspicions of activities seem to be a threat, or a challenge to the traditions of the center, the courts and government are quite willing to abrogate the rights of citizens in the name of some such official proclamation like that of "national security," or the law will be ignored while the police clean out an ideological nest of vipers like the Communist Party of the early fifties or the Black Panther Party of the mid-1960s.

Covert police surveillance can include following a suspect, stake-out, watching the person and premises of a suspect, and also eavesdropping or electronic bugging, wiretapping of telephones, tape recorders, and hidden microphones. The purpose, say the police, is to gather evidence that can help to prevent wrongdoing, stop the ongoing commission of a crime or crimes, or to get information that can be used to prosecute a suspect. The police have at their disposal, for whatever reasons they used them, excellent technology for monitoring citizens and in effect infringing upon their privacy without citizen knowledge. During the 1960s the police in many cities set up intelligence units for the sole purpose of keeping track of certain individuals and groups. This activity had little or nothing to do with preventing the commission of crimes, but it had everything to do with the police being assigned the task of monitoring the movements of suspicious ideological rogues.

The police were actively engaged in many types of operations of this kind to the degree that it frightened the mainstream citizenry, and once again the social center sought to restrict these police activities. In a finding from the case of *Katz* v. *United States,* 1967, the Supreme Court rendered a decision that would seem to place restraints upon this type of police operation.

The police will frequently use undercover agents for surveillance, information, and intelligence gathering. An undercover agent is a law enforcement officer, or someone working for law enforcement, who will mask his identity for the express purpose of deceiving the public. Such deception, say the police, is only used against individuals suspected of or planning a wrongdoing. But a technique such as this is very questionable for law enforcement officers in a free society. The freedom of all citizens is immediately brought into question if we have to conduct our public associations with the thought that friends, neighbors, and strangers may be spies working for law enforcement authorities. The citizenry would become very inhibited about freely expressing themselves. We would live with the fear that practically anything we might do or say could be used against us.

In the case of undercover agents, they have been known to infiltrate organizations and groups, pretending to be a bonafide member. How involved can a police officer become in unscrupulous activities in order to get necessary evidence of criminal, or some other deviant behavior? These are difficult questions for our society to answer. Should an undercover police officer encourage the commission of a criminal act, or any act that would bring police intervention into the exercise? During the active period of a decade and a half ago, law enforcement officers infiltrated many "leftist" and student organizations, and even the Ku Klux Klan. As members of the groups, they encouraged and participated in the commission of unsavory, if not criminal acts. These same police officers were then used as witnesses against those individuals who they had inspired and joined in the commission of acts for which the law was holding the others accountable. This kind of police activity has been styled entrapment, and for years it was used against prostitutes. Entrapment is the act of police officers actually and falsely encouraging a person or persons to break the law.

By using entrapment in such an instance, the police officer can actually become the object of police action and it causes one to wonder whether the act for which the accused is being held accountable would have occurred without the police officer's involvement. Here the police completely step over the bounds of propriety in the legal and moral sense. It is the police who, under false pretenses, draw a citizen into the commission of an illegal act. In entrapment, it is the police who can act as an instigator to the commission of wrongdoing, yet the police can remain blameless.

All of these activities of investigation are therefore for the expressed purpose of seeking to influence and/or take control over an individual or group by the exhibition of a police presence. Even when the arrest procedure is not invoked, the person or group is made aware that they are under surveillance. There are times when the purpose of an investigation is not that of seeking evidence to prosecute, but rather the purpose is that of putting the name or names of individuals in the police files. This clerical procedure is very important to law enforcement work, even when a suspect is released from custody without any formal charge being made against him. If the police make a serious accusation against a person, initially he will be fingerprinted and photographed, and the information becomes a permanent record in the police files of the nation. Perhaps a person is arrested erroneously, still his name is likely to remain in the files for future referral. Once a person is on file, the police will tend to seek him out at their discretion. There have been various attempts to get police to remove these files of people arrested, but not prosecuted for any crime. To this day, however, the police resist doing so. The police are very unwilling to give up the files on people who are poor, black, and of the social fringe, ideologically and otherwise. And frequently such persons are unaware of the fact that they can ask that such a file be destroyed if there is no prosecution flowing from an encounter with law enforcement.

In any event, an encounter with the police, even when the files are destroyed, can be very intimidating in itself to citizens. When the police arrest a person, they take physical charge of him, and at the outset they can treat him like a convicted desperate criminal, handcuffing him and so on. The police have been known to arrest individuals from the social periphery for the specified purpose of intimidating them. It is a way the police caution members of the fringe to stay in their place, and to make no attempt to threaten the social center. As an informal police policy, this action constitutes a form of harassment, but the police say it is just putting the fear of the law in those individuals who might have the inclination to involve themselves in wrongdoing. The television policemen like Kojak often displayed this activity as a means of showing their distaste for the bad guys and the crooks.

Putting the fear of the law into someone is a form of social management. Shading and breaking the law by the police in this effort are justified as a means to a better end. This same "scare um" tactic was used for many years by the police to coerce accused individuals into giving confessions to allegations against them. When the police used these tactics outrageously against blacks and other members of the social fringe during the 1960s, the specter of the brutal cop frightened members of the social center. The law and order crusade could be turned against them. Seeking to protect itself, the social center acted to restrain this type of police tactic.

It was reaffirmed that suspects are presumed innocent until proven guilty. The rights of suspects were not to be abrogated as a matter of their arrest. As part of the law, the principle was established in 1966 with the *Miranda* decision of the Supreme Court *(Miranda* v. *Arizona).* Under this decision it was affirmed that every suspect had a right to remain silent, had a right to a lawyer present during the interrogation concerning the offense for which the individual was arrested, could refuse to answer questions, and the suspect had a right to talk to counsel before being questioned. Each suspect had to be informed of these rights before any interrogation could be made.

Now, the *Miranda* decision sounded very good, but it did not mean very much for the poor, minorities, and fringe group members. Many of these people were not fully aware of the meaning of the *Miranda* decision when they were arrested, and the police frequently did not make the necessary prerequisite statements to inform them of their rights. But even if they were informed, most of them did not have a lawyer to consult about their arrest before police questioning began. The public defender's office tended to be very lax in giving support to suspects who had no other counsel to represent them. And frequently, because of case overloads, the public defender did not get around to seeing the accused until long after the arrest, which meant that the person was held in jail until his rights could be satisfied. The strain of spending time in jail often made the accused more willing to cooperate with the police and the prosecutor's office.

The *Miranda* decision was seen by the police as specifically designed to be helpful to minority suspects, and they opposed the decision. If they carried out the Supreme Court's mandate, they frequently did so in such a slovenly manner that suspects were left uninformed or confused as to the status of their rights at the time of an arrest. To be sure, this seems to occur more with the fringe and minority group citizens than with middle-class whites, if for no other reason than the fact that the police might suspect that middle-class whites would be aware of their rights and they might have a lawyer to back them up.

It is the gulf of suspicion between police and citizenry that spawns protective laws for the rights of suspects. And it was the people of the mainstream who spearheaded the protection and restraints against the police. They did not do it primarily to protect the people of the social fringe, but primarily to protect themselves from possible future police abuse. The police reaction towards these restraints was to describe those of the mainstream who spearheaded such drives as "bleeding heart liberals." This was an obvious comment intended to mean that there were renegades at the social center. These renegades were more concerned with the people who were committing wrongdoing against society than they were concerned with law enforcement officers who were just trying to do their jobs, jobs which also required the police to protect those same liberals from elements of the social fringe.

The police are social managers who readily depend upon their suspicion of the citizenry to help guide them in their work. We are all affected by this force of suspicion that flows from law enforcement. Suspicion is a basic attitude to the social relating in our time. The police inspire it in us, and we, the public, inspire it in them.

JUDGMENTS

Because there is a great deal of suspicion that binds the police and public together, this generates a great need on both sides to be evaluative and judgmental about the other's behavior, as a means of conforming or denying the suspicions they have. This is even more the case for the police because as social managers it is their responsibility to evaluate public behavior. It is the way the police do their job. But it is the way the police do their job that interests the public; which is to say, the public is interested in having an evaluation of the police's evaluation of them. It is like looking at the same situation from two social angles, and one is surely going to get two different perspectives as a result.

For instance, the police tend to see the public as "assholes" who are slow-witted, child-like, and unable to look after their own affairs by and large. This is why they have the police do it for them. They need a strong dominant hand to control and take charge of matters for them. The public tends to see the police as authoritarian personalities who seek out the police role because they love to exercise power over others. Indeed, this belief is one of the reasons why the social center wants to put restraints and checks on the use of police power. The social center sees the police as a necessary evil in a free democratic society.

While there are supportive truths to both these views, they are still basically stereotypical images that are used to confirm, rather than deny, the suspicion of one group towards the other. They form the basis for the justifications that allows one group to view and accept the other in the context in which it is desired. Of course, these stereotypes can come to battle each other as they fight for political acceptance, and they do have concrete reality as it relates to influencing governmental decisions and policy-making.

To be sure the judgment of the police by the public is frequently made in the context of the criminal justice system as a whole, and in recent years there has been a great deal of interest shown in the criminal justice system.

Given the suspicions that exist on an ongoing basis between the police and public, it is not surprising that from this interest has come a great deal of criticism of the criminal justice system, and the system has been attacked by the public as well as the operants and officials of the system itself. Too many criminals are going free, it was said. Strange notions, thought the police, since many of the restraints placed upon them in the 1960s seemed to be designed to accomplish that purpose. Still the police were saying that the system was truncated by "revolving door justice." Furthermore, the courts were singled out as being so weighted down with cases that it made plea-bargaining mandatory. The prisons were seen as being so overcrowded that rehabilitation was impossible and the conditions in the prisons made penal institutions ripe for rape, intimidation, and mayhem that was certain to make the incoming prisoner more hardened in his deviancy. For those who survived the prisons and returned to society, many of them found their way back to prison. Recidivism in our society was of epidemic proportions.

The system as a whole was not doing its job, but it was the police, the frontline troops, who were likely to bear the brunt of criticism because they were familiar and more accessible to public view. Somehow, the quality of the system as a whole was being measured by the public's sense of the quality of police work, as though the police were not only responsible for arresting wrongdoers, but they were also responsible for managing the entire criminal justice system. It was unfair to the police, but when you're passing out blame, fairness is one of the first things that is ignored.

The public was certainly right in many aspects of their criticism of criminal justice and strangely enough the police would readily agree with some of it. They would readily agree with those criticisms that did not directly deal with their functions. The police, like most groups, tend to be protective of their self-image. Therefore, they find no difficulty in agreeing that recidivism is practically of epidemic proportions in our society. It certainly is true that most of the people who are arrested for criminal offenses in large urban centers are likely to spend little or no time in jail. In New York City, for instance, in 1977 more than half of the 225,000 criminal cases were disposed of at arraignment. As an assistant district attorney, working out of Brooklyn, stated in that year, "Out of 80 defendants who take pleas in arraignment here on a given day, 60 would plead guilty to a charge involving little or no jail time. And half of those 60 cases, had the defendant chosen to go to trial (which would involve making bail or waiting in jail until the trial date), would have been dismissed eventually because the complainant wouldn't show, or the evidence would prove weak."[1]

If the criminal justice system is letting most of the apprehended wrongdoers go with little or no time in jail, the truth is that most of the wrongdoers are never caught, say some law enforcement people. The FBI's annual report "Crime in the United States" is a compilation of serious crimes submitted to the bureau by the nation's 11,000 police agencies. This report forms the basis for the crime figures that are usually quoted for the nation.

However, there are many observers of criminal justice who say that the reporting of crime and wrongdoing is not based on clear and consistent statistics. In fact, it is said that there is a great deal of distortion in the statistics that results from an underreporting of crime by local police to the FBI. Recent surveys conducted by the Census Bureau for the Justice Department estimate that for each serious criminal act that is reported, two or three others are not, in part because the victims believe it is futile to file complaints.[2]

At the same time, police departments have increased in size since the explosive 1960s. This growth, backed by public demand, was sought to increase society's fight against crime. But increases in law enforcement personnel and resources have not led to larger increases in prosecutions and convictions of criminals, says a federally funded study of police operations in Washington, D.C. The study found that fewer than ten percent of the police officers on the District of Columbia force made more than half of the arrests that resulted in convictions. One wonders what were the rest of the police officers doing?

The study conducted by the Institute for Law and Social Research in Washington, D.C. stated that in many large cities across the nation, most arrests for serious crimes are either rejected by prosecutors or dismissed after formal charges have been brought. This has special meaning, however, because frequently police performance is measured by the number of arrests officers make, not how many arrests result in convictions.

The study was made under a grant by the Law Enforcement Assistance Administration, and it is the first known, detailed statistical study showing the varying rates of effectiveness of police officers. The study reported that in Washington in 1974 more than half of the 4,347 arrests that ended in convictions were made by 368 officers, or eight percent of the police force. That is to say that fewer than 1,000 officers made arrests that resulted in 84 percent of all convictions.[3]

In search of data to make judgments, no criminal justice area has been free of criticism. In fact, as police departments have grown in size since the 1960s, the public seems to have become even more critical than before of police behavior. This finding resulted from a Louis Harris survey that was done in May of 1977. The survey found that federal law enforcement officials get a 49-39 percent negative rating on their job performance, the lowest recorded by a Harris survey since 1967. This was quite a change from 1970 when a similar survey found that the public approved of federal law enforcement efforts by 60-30 percent. However, by 1975 the earlier positive figure had dwindled to a 44-44 percent standoff.

State law enforcement officials did better than their federal counterparts by scoring a 47-42 percent positive rating. Nevertheless this was down from a 51-39 percent positive rating from a survey conducted two years earlier. The local police forces received a 52-46 percent positive rating. This rating was down from 57-40 percent approval in 1975 and 64-33 percent in 1970.

The Harris survey also found that the public was even more upset at what was seen as the "leniency" of the courts in dealing with criminals. There was 75 percent of the survey that held this view. However, the most disturbing finding was seen in the deep concern the American people had about the effectiveness of their law enforcement system overall. By a 67-16 percent majority, the survey found that the public believed their law enforcement system "does not really discourage people from committing crimes." To be sure, an additional eight percent of the people feel the system actually "encourages crime."[4]

In many respects, these studies of police activities and behavior are specifically ludicrous because they only reflect the beliefs the public has as to the way they would like to see the police system work. After all, the police, the criminal justice system overall, perform very much in a manner that is consistent with society's expectations; which is to say the true expectations the social center has for the police and its encompassing institution. Society's values, principles, its sense of tradition and social conscience has as much to do with the operation of any social institution as the operants who handle it. The condemnation of the criminal justice system by the public is really a condemnation of society; which is to say that the public is condemning itself.

The evaluations of the police and the criminal justice system that have been quoted here are little more than folly. They are made to confirm the suspicions that the social center has, and wants to have, of the police. Members of the social center are very cognizant of the fact that they are dependent upon the police to maintain law and order and the political balance between the center and the social periphery. Perhaps it is the dependency itself which also brings about a need for the evaluation. We do not relish the role, as adults, of being dependent persons.

We feel we must evaluate the police because we know that they are continuously evaluating us. Perhaps there is a sense of getting back at the police through the scientific evaluations of them by pollsters like Louis Harris. If the police are by the nature of their responsibilities given more authority than the citizenry, evaluating them is a way we can try to assert some measure of control over the manner in which they do their job which is managing our daily life affairs.

We make judgments of the police as a means of trying to keep them from over-managing our lives. That the police make counter-judgments against us, shows that there is a battle of judgments going on between the police and the public. Such battling does not help to bring the police and the public closer together, for the ability to form wise opinions tends to be self-righteous in character, and self-righteousness is known to be implacable.

5

POLICE DISCRETION

It was pointed out in chapter 3 of this book that discretionary power is endemic to the criminal justice system and as we have been discussing the system, it could not function in its true role in society without discretion. Because the police play the primary role in the criminal justice system, police discretion has a vital impact on the workings of the entire process. For Jerome Skolnick, police actions, the invoking of the arrest procedure or not, is characterized by arbitrariness, capriciousness, and discrimination. Since it is the police who activate the criminal justice system, their actions and attitudes are then stimulants or likely to be stimulants for the entire system. For instance, if certain individuals or groups are arrested more than others, or citizens are arrested for certain types of crime and not for other types, the system becomes attuned to some individuals and groups as being more deviant than others or certain types of crimes as being more in need of punishment than others, e.g., felony or misdemeanor types of behavioral misconduct.

It is generally believed by the public that the police function in the administration of justice is limited to invoking the criminal process through the arrest procedure. However, studies of police discretion have shown that this narrow role is not followed. For example, in 80 percent of the observed cases, police officers did not arrest law breakers.[1] This would indicate that there is a differential enforcement of the law and this raises serious questions about the "rule of law." As we understand the American legal system, the concept of justice implies conformance to the public expectation of equal allocation of penalties and benefits. This is to say that the operants of the criminal justice system are expected to arrest, defend, prosecute, judge, sentence, and rehabilitate individuals based on the facts of the case alone. Ideally, a person's social, political, economic, or racial characteristics should have no effect on judicial decisions. Given the wide latitude which the police officer possesses in the arrest decision, the ideal is obviated in the first instance.

INFORMAL POLICIES

At the outset, police departments tend to set informal policies for which laws to enforce, how much to enforce them, against whom, and on what occasions.[2] Drinking alcoholic beverages in public, smoking marijuana in public are two instances of law breaking where the police have wide discretionary power. Should they arrest beer drinkers in the park on a Sunday afternoon picnic; should they arrest young people smoking pot as they stroll along the mall in the park? In cases such as these, it is up to the individual police officer, his decision as to what he might do, along with the department's and precinct's policy on such matters, which will be taken into consideration.

In large urban centers where there are many precinct houses, the police frequently will have different policies for administering the same laws, and these policies will be specifically related to race, ethnicity, religion, affluence or non-affluence within the community. Often, these policies will be based upon the police perception of the moral judgments of right and wrong that are understood to exist in a community. Or, the basis could be determined by a political decision from the mayor's office.

The police in local precincts will devise different standards to judge the right or wrong of citizen behavior. They do this more in an attempt to socially manage a community than for the purpose of fighting crime. For example, there can be sharp distinctions made as to which questionable behaviors are acceptable in one neighborhood and not acceptable in another. Drinking alcoholic beverages in public is tolerated much more in poor neighborhoods than in affluent ones. It has been pointed out by social observers that allowing the poor, particularly the blacks, to indulge themselves in alcoholic beverages is part of the means by which the police attempt to control lower-class neighborhoods. An inebriated population on the social periphery is likely to be more destructive of itself than the social center's population. Drunkenness and alcoholism also work to fragment a community if it is present on a large scale. In particular, it will tear at the family unit.

In middle-class white communities, for the same reason, drinking is less tolerated. Society does not want the people of the social center to turn on themselves because it would be the same as turning on society. This concern becomes quite evident with respect to the use and abuse of drugs like marijuana and heroin. To this day, drug use is still largely tolerated in the black and other ethnic communities for the same reason that alcoholic beverages are tolerated. But when middle-class white youths in the 1960s became users and abusers of drugs, the police took up a crusade to rid the communities of the social center of the drug plague, as the public was made to think of it.

The police allow drinking and drugs and gambling openly in the poor communities, but at the same time, when social circumstances dictate, individuals can still be arrested for indulging in allowable violations of the law. The police feel free to arrest wrongdoers of these actions when it suits their purpose.

The social management of these different neighborhood policies was more explicit during the 1960s. For instance, the police were given specific orders by politicians to keep black communities cool and for that reason the police readily tolerated, even more than usual, great numbers of behavior like those just mentioned, and some extraordinary ones. Imagine this, angry black demonstrators were allowed to forcibly imprison public officials in their offices with walk-ins and sit-ins whenever it generally suited their purpose, and it suited their purpose quite often. At the same time, if there were to be more tolerance of deviant, non-conformist acts at the societal periphery, there would be even more tolerance at the social center. Not only was personal drug use by white middle-class youths more tolerated, for example, but an industry sprung up to supply these youths with the drug paraphernalia they needed for these new habits. Head shops appeared across the nation, catering to the middle-class drug trade, middle-class youths could openly smoke pot in movie theaters and at rock concerts, but an individual police officer could still, if he desired, arrest a person for breaking the law in any of these cases. Such informal policies do tend to give the individual police officer greater discretionary power in dealing with individual specific cases, and it allows for greater police capriciousness which is very suitable for the managing of society's various communities.

The police have long had a double standard for enforcement of the law in general as they relate to what has come to be called the law breaking of organized crime and as it would differ with disorganized crime. This is to say that there is believed to be a group of individuals, often called the Mafia, whose lifestyle and normal everyday business involves criminal acts. Widespread gambling, prostitution, and drugs are thought to be under organized crime's control. Their activities are understood to be so sophisticated and embedded in the American culture that for all practical purposes it cannot be rooted out by normal police activities. The police do not ordinarily attempt to control the activities of organized crime, even when it involves murder, except in the most superficial sense. Rarely are gangland type murders ever solved by the police, and the police in New York City actually have an informal policy which states that if the gangsters want to kill each other, let them. Little or no attempt is actually made to try to solve these murders or to root out the widespread nature of organized crime. It is the unorganized criminal or lawbreaker that gets police attention.

It can be understood that organized crime is accepted as a normal part of the American culture by the police. Organized crime may well be a basic institution of American society. Crime and violence is a part of America's tradition. Our nation was built on it in the political and economic sense, and to that degree it could be classified as representing the social center rather than the social periphery. Perhaps this is a reason why institutionalized, organized crime finds itself protected by the inaction of the center's guardians. When members of organized crime are caught, they are likely to receive the same kind of consideration and leniency that other groups of the center receive. This goes right up to the federal government in terms of the Attorney General's office in Washington, D.C. The Justice Department has long been criticized for not investigating more rigorously the activities of organized crime.

The fact that organized crime tends to be viewed as a basic American institution is borne out by the fact that during World War 2, the federal government gave special consideration to Lucky Luciano, the Brooklyn crime boss, while he was in prison, because they wanted him to keep the dock workers in Brooklyn from striking. They knew he had the power to see that strikes did not occur. Later when the Allies were going to invade Sicily, it has been said that Luciano was released from prison with the promise that he would return to Italy and keep his hoodlum friends there from interfering with the Allied invasion plans of that German held island. But more so, the American military wanted his help in preparing the groundwork for the invasion. In more recent years we have information that the Central Intelligence Agency (CIA) solicited help from organized crime in trying to kill Fidel Castro. The point to this is that once again, it can be understood that the chief concern of the police is not crime fighting but rather protection of the central political authority of this country.

Returning to the precincts, the police have always had a great deal of discretion in dealing with complaints that are called into the department. The police decide how they will handle citizen complaints and reports of crime. Their discretion in these matters is supported, unwittingly, by public ignorance and apathy, and the public's perception of their rights to have the police intervene in their affairs.

By and large citizens have only the vaguest understanding of the difference between civil, private, and criminal matters. They call on the police when they are really uncertain of what authority they want the police to act under on their behalf. "Much of their ignorance stems from the belief that they are morally right; therefore, the law is on their side and the police should side with them as complainants, disciplining any errant party."[3] It is left to the police to make an initial evaluation of the calls that come into the department because the department is aware of its limited resources. The police will decide if there is a basis for taking action no matter how urgently assistance is requested.

Citizens are not familiar with the proper way to make a call for assistance, and this encourages the police to make judgments about the calls based on their interpretation of the callers' needs. This brings about an erratic pattern of police response. For instance, the quality of police response to calls for assistance will vary from community to community with respect to the position of that community relative to the social center. There is faster reaction to calls from affluent communities than for communities on the social fringes.

Of course, once a call has been taken by the police and the officers are on their way to the scene of a complaint, the quality of their behavior can vary a great deal depending on the nature of the complaint and their evaluation of it. One of the first determinations to be made is which community issued the call. This is less a problem in the precinct system of large cities because the precinct's location helps to determine from which community came the complaint. In any event, it is the tendency of the police to relax, to take it easy and not to hurry themselves on calls which they judge to be non-serious, often noncriminal matters, which specifically are the types of calls they have to deal with most often in the poorer communities. This raises the question of whether the police are arbitrary in labeling these matters, thereby subverting the goals of citizens' requests in mobilizing the police.[4]

Surely, this suggests that the police, at least in part, are motivated by an impetus of their own which is likely to be based upon their understanding of the police officer's role in America or the customs of their department, the latter more likely being the case. The police will frequently classify calls according to informal, departmental, or precinct policy, and this would likely favor the center communities. It is not favor given as a matter of conscious thought as much as it is a matter of doing what is normally done, but it still results in the use of discretionary power on the part of the police.

There are many factors that go into the police evaluation of complaint calls, and one of the more subtle distinctions that the police make is how much involvement would be required if they do intervene, and even more important, how would the intervention reflect upon the police officers as individuals and as a group.

The police officer, in respect to his person, may be much more concerned with a burglary than with a murder or a rape, although the former will probably get little public attention and the latter will surely receive at least some small coverage in the newspapers. The police officer's concern or lack of it for some crimes versus others is not ordered by indifference or callousness necessarily, or the elevation of property over life. What leads him to this ordering of his concern are his notions about his place on the street which causes him to show a certain kind of discretion towards crime committed on his beat.

For the individual police officer, the most important aspect to a crime can be its setting and this does not refer to the community setting. Crimes are divided by the very simple distinction of "inside" and "outside" crime. The two ideas have little or nothing to do with the legal definitions of private and public places. They derive more specifically from the officer's perception of his work environment. An officer may define a crime as an outside crime when in fact it was committed inside of a building, and an inside infraction may actually have occurred outside on the public streets.

An outside infraction is some wrongdoing that a police officer is expected to be aware of while on his normal patrol. "If a burglar breaks into a building through a rear door or cuts a hole in a roof, his act is considered an inside crime, because the patrol officer had no chance to notice anything amiss, even if he was patrolling alertly. If a person is assaulted in his back yard or mugged in an alley, it is an inside crime, despite its occurrence in a place legally defined as public. But if a burglar breaks open a front door to gain entry, it is an outside crime, because there is no reason why the patrolman should have missed it as he passed (walking or in a squad car). Any outside crime is an affront to the patrolman's notion of himself as a guardian of his territory, an occurrence which suggests to his superiors that he is not doing his work properly."[5]

More interestingly, outside crimes are thought to be more endemic of poor neighborhoods; mugging, purse snatching, and the like, while inside crimes tend to be more endemic of affluent neighborhoods. Police are more anxious to involve themselves in inside crimes. They will respond more readily to calls for assistance for such wrongdoing. This in itself will enhance or detract from the quality of police response to calls for assistance. Discretion in this manner is specifically being used as a defensive type of behavior by the police. They will be more active and aggressive with outside infractions. Such infractions are always viewed as challenges and threats to the responsibilities and authority of the police. Having discretionary freedom in enforcing the laws allows the police to deal more sternly with outside crimes and less sternly with inside infractions.

INTERPRETATIVE POWER

As we readily know the police have ongoing and direct contact with the public in their efforts to maintain law and order. This requires that the police interpret the law when applying it to specific cases. The police must ultimately interpret the law if it is to be used in a practical manner. Police interpretation of the law helps to operationalize its legal authority, and to that degree the legality of the criminal justice system, in terms of all the laws that are administered.[6] For this reason, it can be said that the police become the embodiment of the law, if not the embodiment of the entire criminal justice system. The discretion the police have in interpreting the law at the street level is practically without limits. It is consistent with the fact that in police organizations, discretion increases as one moves down the hierarchy.[7]

The whole basis for police activity, we believe, flows from the authority given them by the law, but if the police can interpret the law at their own discretion, then they constitute, in a large measure, their own authority. It is a bind that is not directly attributable to the police officer in particular, but it is the upshot of a policing system that attempts to govern itself by the rule of law. Laws, in themselves, cannot apply directly to specific cases, but can only be generalized for a category of behavior. The judgment of the police officer is needed in the majority of cases. Only when the wrongdoing is explicit and of the most serious nature are the police not required to manifestly use their judgment in the application of the law.

It is rare for a police officer to be a witness to a crime or infraction. He usually arrives on the scene after the fact and therefore his judgment of the situation becomes crucial to the investigatory steps he must take. The situation becomes even more critical when one understands that each police officer has his own idiosyncratic way of evaluating it, and that includes how he will interpret the law. How one police person handles a situation is not necessarily how another might.

But the power of this becomes even more apparent when it is understood that police interpretation of infractions and the law are likely to influence the district attorney and eventually the judge, if matters go that far, as it might affect the charge, the trial and sentencing. When the situation requires it, the police will file a formal charge against an accused person and this includes a report giving the basis and circumstances for the charge, the interpretation of what happened. It is this interpretation that is used more for the basis of prosecution, than is likely to be the explicit statement of the law. The police interpretation flows from their original evaluation of the situation that led them to make an arrest. The interpretation will most definitely support the actions taken, and not the other way around. This means in effect that the law is used by the police not as a basis for taking action, but more realistically it is used as a justification for actions that have been taken.

The freedom the police have in interpreting the law is clearly seen in the manner in which they can set various policies in different neighborhoods based on the same law. It also tells us that the police can take control of the law, rather than the law controlling the behavior of the police, and in effect, it says that the police make the laws serve their own interests and purpose. It also tells us that if the police genuinely do not want to enforce a certain law, they can easily get away with not doing so, for the patrol officer on the street is generally without a supervisor to watch over him to see that he is upholding his responsibilities. Conversely, it tells us that the police can stretch the law to cover almost any action they may take.

As it relates to normal, day-to-day operations, thanks to freedom of discretion and interpretative elasticity, the police can use their men and resources as they choose most of the time. Inadvertently, however, the covert control that the police can extend over the laws that should guide them makes them more amenable to use by the central political authority for strictly political purposes. No matter what the police are asked to do, there is always a law that justifies their action through its interpretation. This can mean that the police have almost unlimited powers to take actions, when, where, and how they want to. They may be held accountable by a higher authority after actions have been taken, but to prevent them from taking action is just about beyond society's control in the first instance. Society must ultimately rely upon the good judgment of individual officers and not the rule of law which is supposed to guide their behavior.

Because of the relationship of the police to the social fringe, it seems only natural that they would emphasize their work in peripheral communities over the communities at the center. We can see this in the way the police emphasize what they call predatory crimes, crimes against individuals as being more detrimental to society than the more subtle white-collar crimes, when just the opposite may be true. Corporate malfeasance, not only in the stealing of funds but in passing off known dangerous and faulty products to the public, can affect millions of lives. Large chemical companies in the United States have illegally dumped highly toxic chemical waste matter in many residential areas of the country that jeopardizes the lives of millions of people. These acts are not exploited by the police or the press as much as "predatory crimes," but as white-collar crimes they are more dangerous to society.

It is the police who can and do decide to what degree they will enforce the law. Laws, in and of themselves, are not self-enforcing, and because the law rarely if ever coincides exactly with real life situations or with the temper of the community at a given moment in history about the seriousness of an offense, judgment would seem to be required in their application. Police officers not only have to decide if a law has been broken in order to invoke the criminal justice process, but they frequently have to decide if the law has been sufficiently violated to warrant arrest and punishment.

There are many different factors the police may use in deciding whether or not to invoke the criminal justice process. These factors can be quite extraneous to the strict canons of the law. Take the factor of public morality, which among other things is perceived by the police as varying from community to community; public morality may be taken into consideration when a decision to arrest is to be made. Not only is there the morality of the community to be considered, but there is the morality of the police officer himself.

This factor of morality can be understood in the following light. Particular to a given community, the citizens there may think that it is wrong for a wife and children to pay twice for a husband's drunkenness. The reasoning could go like this: it is bad enough that a husband may squander the meager livelihood of the family, but why compound the harm by arresting the man and depriving the family of all support. Further, the public tends to have a more forgiving nature towards wrongdoers during certain times of the year, like Christmas and New Year holidays. It is believed that people should be given a little extra leeway during these periods.

It is also considered to be right and proper that roughnecks and bullies should be treated more severely than others.[8] This conviction has wide ramifications for the police role. Society takes this view and applies it to whole communities. The bully is an unrestrainable individual, by his own actions. He is a menace to society because of it. He needs close supervision and authoritarian control. When the same kind of description is placed upon whole communities, the same reasoning follows, and there is the police to place the authoritarian control over groups of bully citizens.

Bullies tend to be social outcasts, fringe members of society, and so the reasoning goes for those communities that are also given the same descriptive titles. Society expects the behavior of the police to be more aggressive in bully communities. It is justified on the grounds that the police are living up to one aspect of the implicit morality of our society.

Police departments will set policies that will require individual officers to use their discretion if those policies are to be implemented. Administrative prerogatives are in themselves acts of discretion, and the concerns of police administrators frequently can have more to do with the techniques of administration and the political milieu; administrators are prone to make policies that serve administrative needs, and these policies often do not meet the needs of the beat patrolman in his effort to enforce the laws. Administrators are likely to interpret the law to suit their purpose.

Therefore when a precinct commander orders his men to treat hippies with courtesy and respect and to let them use the local parks without disturbance by the police; or when administrators decide to saturate a particular community with foot patrol officers; or when the police commissioner decides that a fourth platoon is needed, the purpose of which is the better deployment of forces during the more difficult periods of the day, these are all exercises in police discretion at the administrative or command level.[9] Discretion at the administrative level is likely to be strongly motivated by political and management realities but not the practicalities of day-to-day law enforcement.

If I can harken back to something that was pointed out earlier to better join the connection here of political influence over the use of police discretionary powers, it is the top political office of the city that can have the most direct influence over the use of administrative discretion by the police, and this is the mayor's office. The most potent force the mayor has in this regard relates to that portion of his budget that is allowed for the police department under him. This allocating factor will easily determine the manpower of the department, the types of equipment that will or can be purchased, and it speaks of the level of wages and pensions for the officers. It may also help to determine what civilians will enter the department as recruits.

Further, the mayor's office is a conduit for public opinion as to the kinds of law enforcement the public wants. "Does the public want prostitutes chased, arrested, or tolerated? Is the traffic situation serious enough to warrant $10.00 tickets or a towaway program? Do the residents of the Upper West Side really need the additional police protection for which they have been clamoring?"[10]

The interpretative powers of the police, from the administrators down to the foot police officers, are immense. They interpret the law, public behavior, the sense of public morality, and the degree to which a behavior is considered to be vile enough to require the full invocation of the criminal process.

It could be said that the use of discretionary powers by the police is an attempt, in part, to free themselves from the restraints of strictly following the canons of the law. At the same time, it could be said that in breaking the law the public may be attempting to free itself from the restrictions of the laws that threaten them. As the police represent the physical presence of the law, breaking the law is also an attempt by the individual citizen to free himself from the police, in the sense that the police stand for the maintenance of the law.

It is probably fair to say that the police use their discretion to strengthen their position as a social group in society relative to other groups. They are greatly influenced in this effort by politicians, by the community, by many factors, but overall they may be governed most by the pure sense of survival as a social entity, which is precisely, or may be precisely, the extent of the governing motivations for politicians, the citizenry, and society overall.

The discretionary power of the police does not in the first instance flow from the fact of individual judgments per se, but results from the fact that society has determined, either by design or accident, that our social system should have a policing policy that requires the use of a high degree of discretionary power. It starts from the outset with the laws that empower the police to exist. The laws must be interpreted to be activated, and when they are interpreted by the police and other operants of the criminal justice system, this causes a buildup of discretionary power.

The entire criminal justice system is based on the use of discretionary powers, and this follows from the true role that the police and the system are being asked to follow. We as members of society, have chosen to relinquish our responsibility to maintain social order through our own individual efforts. We have chosen to delegate that authority to a specific group of citizens whom we have elevated to a power position over us. But this has, in effect, created a source of disequilibrium within the society and therefore makes it more difficult for social order to be obtained.

We gave the police the authority to maintain law and order and in the process we gave them the right to interpret the law and use the power of discretion and judgment that came with it. Since the police are the principal activators of the criminal justice system, their judgments and influence ripple throughout the entire process. The justice system depends upon the police to make things happen, and this enhances police discretionary powers.

But it all works out very well in the end for society as a whole; for a policing system that has a great deal of discretionary power is one that can easily be used for the many facets of social management which is the basic police function. That the police also catch criminals is perhaps a happenstance rather than a purpose. The police and the criminal justice system exist because of social management policies rather than the other way around. A balance must be kept that favors the social center over the social periphery, and it is the police that act as society's fulcrum.

CONCLUSIONS

I have in my memory an experience that is as fresh as though it happened only this morning. It is an event that occurred 38 years ago, but the years in between have not dimmed the image. It happened when I was five years old on a hot summer afternoon within the interior of my home. I was sitting in the kitchen with my mother when there was a knock at our front door. My mother, as was her habit, rose and went to the hallway that led from the kitchen to the front door and asked the caller to come in. The door was roughly thrown open with a bang against the hall's wall, and an angry looking policeman stepped through the opening and hurried to where my mother was standing.

I recognized the policeman right away. He normally patrolled our neighborhood, but this was the first time he had ever come into my home. Stopping before my mother with a snarl on his face, he asked for two of my older brothers by name. My mother replied that she did not know at that moment where they were and that she had not seen them all afternoon. As my mother finished with her statement, the policeman with his gun hanging low at his side and his nightstick hanging from a loop over his left arm, went into a rage, screaming at my mother that she was lying and he wanted my two brothers brought to him immediately.

My mother flinched and withdrew a little, but repeated what she had said previously. The police officer shook his finger in her face and screamed louder than before, demanding even more authoritatively that my brothers be brought to him instantly. My mother was becoming increasingly frightened because the police officer would drop his hand

112

to his gun between the times he wasn't shaking his finger in her face. I too was feeling extremely frightened, for I had seen enough movies even at that age to know the power of a pistol.

My mother backed away from the officer and started to enter the kitchen, probably to come to my side and comfort me from this rather violent verbal scene. But as she did so the policeman went into what looked like an uncontrollable rage. He screamed louder than before and grabbed my mother about the neck and began to choke her. I screamed at that point "Mommy! Mommy! Mommy!" But the police officer was oblivious to me, and he continued to choke my mother who was now crying and gasping for breath under the weight of this man's crazed fingers.

What could I do? I wanted to help my mother, but I kept looking from the policeman's choking hands to the gun hanging at his side, and the alternating sight immobilized me. I started to pee and scream louder "Mommy! Mommy! Mommy!"

At some point the policeman seemed to come to his senses, and he released his grip on my mother's throat. She almost collapsed to the floor, but stumbled her way over to me, where she quickly took me up in her arms. Barely able to speak, she was trying to tell me that everything was all right and not to be frightened.

The police officer stood in the hallway staring at us as though he was trying to fathom what had gotten me so upset, and the realization of what he had just done seemed to suddenly come over him. As it did, he abruptly turned and left our house quickly, leaving an open front door behind him.

My mother soon stopped my tears and trembling, trying to explain to me that everything was all right, and the whole matter was nothing but a mistake. But as well as I could remember, it took a very long time for the immediate fear that had lodged inside of me to recede, and it has never really gone away, for I saw the exercise of raw power, police power, and I have always been shy of police officers as a result.

My mother never did find out what had brought on this violent encounter with the policeman. She questioned my brothers when they returned home but they could shed no light on it. She went to the precinct house to make a formal complaint against the officer, but she was not well received. However, the policeman did disappear from our neighborhood. I don't think I ever saw him again, but he was never to be forgotten. More importantly, I recognized from that time forward that the police represented unfettered power that could be released at any time, at their discretion, with a fist, the nightstick, or the pistol. I grew up with the feeling that the police were a personal threat to me, not to mention my mother, brothers, and sisters, and I lived with the dread that the knock at the door would someday come again and there would be the angry face of that police officer or some other police officer, ready to do bodily harm to my family or myself.

To transpose my childhood experience to this discussion, I honestly believe that all of us live in America with the feeling that the police are an implied threat to civil society of which we are a part. I think we all live with even a sense of dread, no matter how remote, that the police officer may come knocking at our door someday and we may fall under the control of the criminal justice system. I do not think that this is an exaggerated proposal. The public's attitude with all its talk of being dependent upon the police to protect it from deviant and criminal elements, show many signs of being weary of the presence of an armed group in society, whose sole purpose is that of monitoring our behavior and making judgments about our social conduct.

The fear of the police is at the social center. It is the center that has attempted through the courts and laws to place restraints upon the authority and power of the police. These actions, dealing with frisking, search and seizure, and surveillance attempt to curtail the police's ability to initiate actions against the public at their own capriciousness and whim. There is the feeling that the police are always ready to pounce on the citizenry as a matter of their job. We tend to withdraw from them. We don't make friends with them easily, and we tend to feel uncomfortable around them. As they tend to be suspicious of us, so are we in turn.

Our society has created an unusual situation for itself that is inconsistent with earlier Western social tradition. In large measure we have given up our rights to look after our own behavior. Social order once manifested itself through a sense of individual moral consciousness and obligations to others and society. But we have given up this individual responsibility and allocated it to an armed body of individuals we deem as the police. But in doing so, we have tacitly dubbed ourselves as people who are unwilling or unable to maintain the social order; we have to be coerced by laws and symbolically threatened by the nightstick and the gun in order for us to maintain the norms of interacting behavior. We acknowledge, unlike the philosophers of the Enlightenment period, that people are not basically good, but probably bad, devious, plotting, and perhaps continuously looking for ways to subvert their neighbors. We are animals in the worst sense and without the police, lawlessness and anarchy would reign because we cannot control ourselves and love our brothers.

We have created a social institution and made it in the Orwellian sense our *big brother*. But as it can often be the case with siblings, we are not entirely comfortable with the relationship because big brothers have the tendency to dominate and flex their muscles to the negation of the wishes of little brother. The police, as big brother, are our society's principal instrument for social management. They are supported by a whole raft of government mechanisms that exist to intervene in our lives, protect us, to take control of us.

The coming of modern society, with its scientific predilection, has rationalized our social life, and to that degree, dehumanized us. As we have discovered natural laws of the physical sciences, we have come to think that there are natural laws that can also define, predict, and control, when used properly, human behavior. A sense of morality is too abstract for the running of a modern complex society based on science and technology. We believe the citizenry can be controlled by applying the general law to specific cases, but we have the tendency to forget that people are not just organic chemicals that can be manipulated in a flask or a test tube over a bunsen burner.

The scientific attitude is by its nature a conservative one, and the laws that have been devised by politicians to govern society follow this pattern. Maintaining law and order then becomes a system of validating those social values and beliefs that have come to be accepted as truths according to tradition, and they ultimately restrict the liberal tendency that gave birth to the democratic principles which are thought to be at the basis of the political nature of our society. There is an inherent tension in a social system that attempts to maintain law and order by the use of a police force, while also attempting to implement democratic principles.

Laws are but general prescriptions, whatever the political reasoning that brought them into existence. They represent a sense of the collective rather than the individual will and spirit, in the final analysis. Therefore by trying to govern the social order by law, the individual will is sacrificed to the abstract concept of the group will. This point of view flows directly from the ideology of democracy. Consequently, what the laws cannot do, in and of themselves, we rely upon the police to do. They are expected to make the citizenry conform as individuals. This makes the law and the police restricters of individual freedom, and for the individual citizen, the police symbolize this reduced freedom.

As laws represent a social tradition, the citizens who are willing to abide by those traditions are in the end more favored by the laws. The polity of the nation is based around these social traditions, and the laws of the land tend to support and protect such traditions. The citizens who come under this favored mantle receive special consideration and support from the institution which has been given the responsibility for maintaining the laws, the criminal justice system. The citizens who are not favored, for whatever the reasons, are likely to be in disfavor with the criminal justice system. This is to say that the criminal justice system, the policing system of America, specifically works to maintain the status quo, for that encompasses the core of this nation's social traditions.

For a society that professes to be both liberal and specifically democratic, the concept of the status quo cannot possibly contain the ideologies of all its people, at all times in history. Indeed, the concept flies in the face of the system's credo of freedom for all, and it can be a stagnant element for society and culture as a whole. Therefore our society finds itself in the posture of continually trying to maintain the status quo by maintaining a balance between the political and ideological forces of society. Relying on the law to govern behavior and influence attitudes, the police find themselves being used as a tool to maintain this balance. This is not a decision that is made by the police themselves, but rather it is made by the central political authority of society that has given the police this mandate.

As the needs of society change, as social and historical perspectives change, so change the demands citizens will make upon the society, in particular the government. New social forces and ideologies must inevitably arise as a result, and amidst this, the police must continually maneuver to maintain their mandate of keeping the balance of political forces in favor of the social center. It clearly points up the fact that the police are a manipulable political tool that works for the government, and not necessarily, if at all, for the public.

As scientism requires a rational reasoning mind, so it is believed that democracy in the modern state form requires rational conduct in political affairs. We must be able to reason together to make acceptable decisions for ourselves. If our belief systems, our sense of values, are too divergent, then reasoning together becomes an impossible task. The status quo is justified on the basis that it can support consensus, and the balance of political forces must be weighed in favor of the status quo for the success of a consensual political system. This puts the police in a position of favoring strongly one group or some group over others. The police watch over and scrutinize the citizenry for the sake of the polity and government, rather than for the sake of the citizens themselves.

The police then cannot be impartial or chiefly concerned with criminals as we would normally want to believe. Instead, they must be concerned with the social dissidents who might undercut the values and traditions that have come to represent the social center and thereby help to maintain the status quo. The police's immediate attention is drawn to nonconformity, any action or behavior that can spite the norms of the social center. This puts every citizen under the purview of the police, and makes us all potential suspects and possible dissidents in their eyes.

There are whole categories of Americans who fall into this posture of being dissidents because they have been allocated certain statuses outside of the mainstream of society in accordance with our stratification system. These people are nonconformists because society will not allow them to conform. Being recognized as social dissidents, the ethnic minorities are expected to fall sharply under police scrutiny and observation. These are groups who are hesitant in their collective will to conform because society has discriminated against them and denied them equal opportunity. They want to change their position in society which makes them a force that is attempting to liberalize the polity and weaken the social traditions that have denied them an equal place in society. They are a force that wants to encroach upon the social center and therefore they are perceived as a threat to the balance of political forces that are needed for the consensus polity and the maintenance of the status quo.

The social center and the police as a result find themselves in a position that socially requires them to oppose these groups. There is no place at the center for them because status-wise they are deemed different and unworthy. Therefore, the police are used to keep them on the social periphery for the good of society as a whole. The needs of the social center must take precedence over the deprivations that may befall them. This is particularly true as it relates to any of these fringe, social groups being able to obtain a true measure of political power. For this reason, police activities will tend to rise during those periods when the groups of the social periphery are socially active, e.g., the 1960s, because their activities will be perceived as attempts to gain greater political power. This is an unwanted occurrence because it would bring them into direct social intercourse at the social center. Such a development would overthrow the balancing mechanism that is thought necessary to the consensus polity. Our society cannot, or will not, allow this to happen.

Having now completed this discussion on the policing of America, one final essential point needs to be made. Our social system has established a mechanism for the policing of society under the belief that such a mechanism is necessary and viable to the maintenance of social order. On both accounts this assumption may be genuinely misguided, if not entirely incorrect. The arguments against this have already been given, but it needs to be further pointed out that our policing mechanism serves to maintain a series of abstract notions of justice and the societal good. These ideas tend not to be logical or rational, i.e., the scales of justice always even out in the end; yet these same ideas purportedly form the basis for a rational legal system that is instrumental to the operations of the criminal justice system. This in itself suggests that there is a hidden agenda at work in our justice system, and that the policing of America serves some unspecified ends.

The fact that we are so willing to refer to criminal justice as the guardian of the scales of justice, the rule of law, and other unfathomable social ideals attest to the misconceptions we have about the core of our nation's policing policy.

The academicians and professionals who study the criminal justice system, by and large take for granted that the primary purpose of the system is that of maintaining law and order. Their mind-set holds that this premise is not to be challenged, and as a consequence, in my opinion, it has helped to greatly limit our understanding of the justice system and the policing of America. I hope this book, if nothing else, brings into question that mind-set. Society is best served by an inquiring mind rather than a closed one.

NOTES

CHAPTER 2: MAINTAINING THE STATUS QUO

1. Edward Shils, "Theory of Mass Society," *Diogenes* (1962), pp. 53–54.
2. Allan Silver, "The Demand for Order in Civil Society," *The Police*, ed. by David J. Bordua (New York: John Wiley, 1967), pp. 1–24

CHAPTER 4: THE POLICE AND SOCIETY

1. *New York Post*, "Bargaining Crime Away," January 10, 1979, p. 25.
2. *New York Times*, "Fuzzy Crime Statistics," Section 4, September 18, 1977.
3. ———, "Police Study Views Law Conviction Rate," September 19, 1977.
4. *New York Post*, "Poll: Police are not Effective," May 12, 1977.

CHAPTER 5: POLICE DISCRETION

1. Donald J. Black, "Police Encounters and Social Organization: An Observational Study" (Ph.D. diss., University of Michigan, 1968).
2. Kenneth Culp Davis, *Police Discretion* (St. Paul, Minnesota: West Publishing Company, 1975).
3. Albert J. Reiss, Jr., *The Police and the Public* (New Haven: Yale University Press, 1971), p. 77.
4. Ibid., p. 76.
5. Jonathan Rubinstein, *City Police* (New York: Ballantine Books, 1977), pp. 341-2.
6. Jerome H. Skolnick, *Justice Without Trial* (New York: John Wiley, 1966), p. 246.
7. James Q. Wilson, *Varieties of Police Behavior* (New York: Atheneum, 1975), p. 7.
8. David H. Bayley and Harold Mendelsohn, *Minorities and the Police* (New York: Free Press, 1968).
9. Alexander B. Smith and Harriet Pollack, *Crime and Justice in a Mass Society* (San Francisco: Rinehart Press, 1973), p. 109.
10. Ibid., p. 126.

INDEX

Beame, Abraham, 89
Beatniks, the posturing of new lifestyles, 31
Black Americans, as serfs, 19; the
protest movement of the 1960s, 24;
as nonconformist on the social
periphery, 33-39; political power,
35; youthful offenders, 58-59; the
perpetrator, 71; tolerated behavior,
102
Black Panthers, miscarriages of justice,
44; community relations offices, 87;
search and seizure, 91
Bruce, Lenny, 44
Bureaucracy, abstract authority, 16

Capitalism, the values of, 17-18
Centralized government, in America
today, 27-28
Chicago Police riots, unchecked use of
police authority, 89
Community of institutionalized
deviancy, defined, 34
Community relations offices, of the
police, 86
Consensus model, of political decision-
making, 22-24; government use of
28; police maintenance of, 29;
politics of moderation, 32
Conservative politicians, belief in the
negative character of people, 6;
support of the police, 6; balancing
political forces, 32
Correctional officers, as jailers, 64-65

Cricket, Jiminy (conscience), 82
Crime, inside and outside, 105
Crime statistics, underreporting, 97
Criminal justice system, explained, 41;
the administration of justice, 49;
parole board, 68; cynicism, 69;
ongoing struggle between contending
social forces, 70; plea-bargaining, 73;
government and politics, 75
Cynicism, an accepted social view, 69

Davis, Angela, 44
Decentralized governance, under
feudalism, 26-27
Democracy, defined, 22-25; social
protest, 75-76
Diversity, of modern urban life, 20
Durkheim, Emile, 5, 7

Family, as a social welfare unit, 14
Federal governmental system, defined,
27
Feudalism, the breakdown of traditional authority, 13; class structure,
13-14; land wealth, 26

Garvey, Marcus, 36

Harris, Louis, 98
Headshops, used by the youths of the
social center, 102
Hippies, the posturing of new life-
styles, 31
Hoover, Edgar J., 37

www.ingramcontent.com/pod-product-compliance
Lightning Source LLC
Chambersburg PA
CBHW020254290526
45784CB00003B/1253